Christine Learoyd was born in 1941 in Canterbury, Kent. The memory of her deeply unhappy childhood made her promise that when she had children of her own they would never have to suffer the tension and trauma of parental fights and arguments. At the age of seventeen she trained as a nurse at the Royal Sea Bathing Hospital in Margate. It was there that she met her husband, Fred, who was a regular visitor to his sick mother, a patient in Christine's ward. That same year they were married, and two years later, after they had moved to Germany where Fred was serving in the Army, she gave birth to her first child, Kevin, who was followed by Stephen and Lorraine. Today Christine is a grandmother four times over and a devoted mother to her adopted and fostered handicapped children.

Jane Owen was born in London and brought up near Windsor. After a year spent working as a teacher at Clyde School in Australia, made famous by the film 'Picnic at Hanging Rock', she read Late Ancient and Medieval History at London University and subsequently became a journalist. Almost every national newspaper has publisher her work on subjects as diverse as the English legal system and St Valentine's Day, and she has written several books. She is joint winner of the Van den Berghs and Jurgens reporting award. Today she is Editor of the 48 Hours section of the Daily Express and also writes the Daily Express gardening column.

MATTHEW

My Son's Struggle

Christine Learoyd
with Jane Owen

Futura

A *Futura* Book

ISBN 0 7088 4530 4

Typeset in Palatino by Fleet Graphics, Enfield, Middlesex

Reproduced, printed and bound in Great Britain by
BPCC Hazell Books
Aylesbury, Bucks, England
Member of BPCC Ltd.

Futura Publications
A Division of
Macdonald & Co (Publishers) Ltd
Orbit House
1 New Fetter Lane
London EC4A 1AR
A member of Maxwell Macmillan Pergamon Publishing Corporation

CONTENTS

ACKNOWLEDGEMENTS

I want to thank Matthew for choosing us, for changing our lives and taking us on such marvellous adventures. We owe him a lot, and we owe a great deal to all those people who have made his dream a reality. Thousands of people all over the world have helped our son although many of them have never met Matthew, Fred or me. We do not even know the names of several hundred people who sent donations or gave moral and practical support to Matthew anonymously. But here is my opportunity to say thank you, again.

Professor Ian Jackson is one of the most modest men I know and no doubt he will be embarrassed to see his name in print so many times in this book, but he deserves a special thank you, as do the trustees of Matthew's fund – A.R. Daly (Chairman), S.W. Weaver (Secretary and Treasurer), J.K. Dyer, C.G. Goodwin and R. Monk – and the National Westminster Bank, Walmer Branch, which looks after the fund.

My heartfelt thanks also to Bob Monk; fire-fighters on both sides of the Atlantic; the Scouting organizations here and in the United States; Christine Piff; Hadi Argent of Parents for Children; Vivienne; the *People*; TVam; News at Six; TVS; Invicta Radio; the *Mercury* newspaper in Kent; the *Deal Express*; David

Graves of the *People*; all the family, especially my daughter Lorraine who has taken on all the menial tasks of nappy-changing and cleaning up; the people of Rochester in the USA; Alan Samson of Queen Anne Press.

And my love and thanks to Fred for standing by us come hell or high water.

Christine Learoyd

MATTHEW

At the end of 1982 our son Steve wrote from Germany to say that the Army had given him leave to take a holiday back in England in three weeks' time. This was good news; we hadn't seen him for over six months, and since his posting to Germany – his first after completing his training in Aldershot – we hadn't heard much from him. Like most lads of his age he is not a good letter-writer, so I was looking forward to catching up with all his news. Just as I was telling my husband, Fred, about Steve's planned visit Matthew came into the sitting-room, and the sight of him made my heart sink. How could I tell an eight-year-old boy who had spent most of his life in a long-stay hospital that after three months with us he might have to leave? That had always been the plan, because we were merely a 'bridging' family for him while social workers tried to find him a permanent niche in a family; but Matthew had settled into our lives far more readily than we had expected. Steve's homecoming forced the issue because Matthew was sleeping in Steve's bed, and there simply wasn't room for them both.

It was as if life was set against Matthew. He was born so disfigured and with such unusual medical problems that he was abandoned at birth and kept in hospital until only a few months before we met him for the first time. I wished that we were in a position to help him but we weren't, so it was best to remind him right away that he would soon be moving to another family. I tried to sound positive. I told Matthew how pleased we were that Steve was coming home, and said that the adoption agency was bound to have found him a lovely family where there were fewer children, so there would be more care, attention – and even toys – for him. With our own three grown-up children away from home, and five fostered and adopted physically and/or mentally handicapped children to care for, we weren't able to give Matthew as much time as we would have liked.

For someone who cannot move his eyes and lips in the way most of us can to show our emotions, Matthew's face is extraordinarily expressive – to those who know him, anyway. His face was a picture of unworried trust. 'It's OK,' he said. 'I'll sleep on the floor when Steve comes home.'

And that was how Matthew adopted us. Oh, it didn't happen right away – it took several weeks of heart-searching on both sides, a year or so of bureaucratic toing and froing, and several mountains of paperwork – but in retrospect that was the moment when our fates were welded together, because Matthew had made up his mind. He had also captured our love so firmly that even if he hadn't said he would stay, I don't think we could have let him go in the long run. The strangest part of it was that only five months earlier when I first laid eyes on Matthew – a picture of him, in fact – I was so horrified by his face that I turned away and said to Fred, 'Poor little boy, I could never love a boy like that.' Fred had asked to see the picture. The face that stared back wasn't much like any human face. The photograph showed a large skull, a few wisps of black hair, no ears, a misshapen gash for a mouth which extended far across the face, a tiny nose, grotesquely swollen, watery, red eyes with such dark skin around them that he looked vaguely like a panda. He also had webbed fingers frozen in a permanently bent position and skin so dry that it cracked and bled whatever we tried. There was worse, as we were to learn: Matthew had one or two internal problems which could, unless sorted out, affect his development.

We had been sent his picture and a brief summary of his background by an adoption agency called Parents for Children, which is based in Camden Town, London, and aims to find homes for children who are difficult to place. Like all the children included on their list, Matthew had written a brief account of his own needs and dreams – it made poignant reading. Matthew said he would like a mummy and daddy, brothers and sisters, a dog and lots of cuddles. Parents for Children were determined to fulfil his dreams. No challenge is too great for them, as Matthew's case demonstrated, but we decided that he was too big a challenge for us. Until Hadi Argent, our social worker from Parents for Children, rang one misty day in October.

Could we take Matthew in temporarily until after Christmas? Could we be a 'bridge'? He had been moved from a long-stay hospital for mentally and physically handicapped children in the Home Counties, where he had spent his early years up until the age of about seven, to a prospective adoptive home. She explained that unfortunately it had taken only six weeks for the parents and Matthew to decide that they had not been well matched: Matthew's first experience with a real family had not worked out. Hadi explained that Matthew was very concerned about how Father Christmas would find him if he moved again, and he wanted to know where he would spend his eighth birthday, in November. The

11

experience had been traumatic for Matthew because his first taste of 'normal' family life had failed. He had been rejected, and now this frightened, bemused child needed a home where he could stay for three months and rebuild his confidence before taking his next step into permanent family life.

I find it hard to turn children away and, without letting myself consider the practicalities too deeply – without even speaking to Fred – I said, 'Yes'. Hadi reminded me that this was the terribly disfigured boy who had featured regularly in the Parents for Children news-sheet. I heard my voice saying, 'Yes, I know which one he is. We'll take him until the New Year.' There are never any fixed dates for bridging families and their charges, we just learn to live from day to day, fitting in with what the adoption agencies want and what we, the bridging family, can manage. I decided that we would be able to cope for three months.

Quite clearly, I had gone mad. That was the only explanation. How would we cope with his grotesque appearance? How would friends, neighbours and their children react to his appearance? I lit a cigarette, walked through to our kitchen to make a cup of coffee and looked through to the bathroom where a row of five hooks, each with a child's name, carried five brightly-coloured face flannels. Soon there would be a sixth. How would we manage yet another child in our three-bedroomed council semi? Well, it was called a three-room semi, but it was more of a two-bed semi with a box room. Thank heavens for the person who invented bunk beds – without his brainwave we would never have managed. The house was the end of a block of three, in Aylesham, Kent; it was only a few years old and it was light and airy. We were very happy there although space, or lack of it, was a problem. That was one of the reasons I hesitated before accepting Matthew, but when I said 'Yes' to

Hadi there was no going back; I was scared – and excited. But I like and need these challenges.

Fred arrived back from his mining shift at the Snowden Pit at two o'clock and spotted the bright yellow pages of the Parents for Children news-sheet lying open on the table. 'Having a clear out?' he asked casually. We can read each other's minds and he knew already that I had accepted a new child, but I suppose he was hoping against all the odds that I hadn't committed us to yet another one. I owned up – after all, I said to Fred, how could we say no? Fred never says much: he's a typical man and doesn't like showing his emotions. Anyway, he said he supposed that if he refused I would lock him in the garden shed. I said I would, so he replied, 'There you are, I'd better say yes then.' He isn't really henpecked, but he likes to imagine he is. It was a Wednesday, and Fred had been looking forward to a restful weekend. Instead, he would have to crank up our old banger, a bronze-coloured Hunter, and drive the three hours to London to meet the new addition. The journey should take only one and a half to two hours, but I get so carsick that it usually took far longer. Thank heavens for Fred's good temper. In the end he laughed and joked and said he would get out the spare tube of glue to hold the car together for the trip.

At tea-time a local authority bus brought our assortment of adopted and long-term foster children back from their special school. We settled down to spaghetti on toast, some cake and pots of tea as they burbled about what they had been doing all day. After tea they trooped into the sitting-room as they always do to play or watch television. We told them to be quiet so that we could give them some news. We explained who Matthew was and why he needed a home and some loving brothers and sisters for three months. Then we showed them his picture. There was silence. And that

13

is unusual in our household. Finally there was a burst of questions about Matthew, punctuated by Ben who demanded to know when everyone would stop talking so that he could watch his favourite programme. Then Ben added, 'Oh, he's black like Sarah.' In fact, both Sarah and Matthew are of mixed race. One child wanted to know what had happened to Matthew's face: was it squashed or burned – what had happened? We explained that Matthew was born with an almost unknown disease called Ablepheron Macrostomia Syndrome; it was a label but not much more, and it was about as much as anyone could give by way of explanation – even the doctors were puzzled by Matthew's strange condition. The explanation was accepted. Another child wanted to know about his toys. Then Lorraine, our natural daughter who has two children of her own but still helps with our crowd, said she was frightened she wouldn't be able to look at him. Our natural son Kevin, who had popped in for tea, was more forthright. He said he was not going to get involved. It was not an encouraging beginning. We thought that Matthew would be gone before our son Steve returned from Germany, but although the temporary addition hardly affected him we wrote to tell him a bit about Matthew.

We left the kids to their games and went off to try to convince each other that we had done the right thing, and that we would be able to cope. Sleep didn't come easily that night. In the morning we packed the kids off to school, arranged for a friend to stop by in case the children arrived back before we did, and headed for Camden Town. The journey, made longer by carsickness stops, took over four hours. Parents for Children is housed on the High Street and has a bright yellow front with shop windows showing photographs of children in need of families and homes. It makes a change from window displays of designer

14

durables! Inside, Hadi and Phillida, Matthew's social workers, welcomed us and showed us to armchairs around a small coffee table where a file containing Matthew's details lay.

Matthew was born to a white Irishman and a black woman. His appearance at birth was so horrifying that he was abandoned; and he was not expected to live beyond a few months. He had to be fed through a tube into his stomach. I suppose it was because his 'mouth' was so wide that he wasn't able to suck; but I had no way of knowing definitely because adoptive parents are not always given detailed medical records other than those about the child's current state of health. The files explained that, as the months passed and Matthew clung to life, the hospital decided on one or two more operations to make his disfigured body more functional. He had no eyelids, so they grafted skin around his eyes to form lids and to save his already poor eyesight. They reduced the size of the gaping slit which served as a mouth to give him a better chance of feeding properly, and they carried out one or two more operations to improve his digestive system. He defied all expert predictions and survived, although his development was so slow that no one could be sure whether he had a mental handicap. It was decided to keep him in a long-stay hospital in the Home Counties, and he stayed there for seven years. Despite the fact that he had never had a family he never felt deprived, or so he says now. In fact, Matthew says he was happy. His happiness had a lot to do with a nurse called Vivienne, who took a special interest in him. Vivienne gave up much of her spare time to try to give Matthew plenty of 'normal' experiences: she would take him home to stay with her at weekends, introduce him to other children of his age, take him shopping, and just give him as much love and attention as she could.

Over the years as Matthew grew up society's attitude to handicapped people changed. Many more ordinary families were adopting handicapped children, and the hospital where Matthew lived began to feel that perhaps he, too, should be put forward for adoption. The regular adoption channels probably would not have been able to place him, so he was put on the books of Parents for Children. Every now and then they put out a newsletter – the one with yellow pages that I have already described – and it was through the newsletter that three couples came forward to care for Matthew. The first two dropped out because they felt, as soon as they looked through the details of Matthew's life, that he was not right for them, but the third welcomed him into their family only to find that their life and Matthew's had nothing in common. We heard, with sinking hearts, that Matthew had great difficulty in fitting in with family life. It was hardly surprising that he had problems because he had no idea how a family worked – after spending all his life in hospital he was completely institutionalized. His stay with his first family had brought to light many nasty traits: he was spiteful; he used his looks to scare the younger children into submission; he was very greedy for toys, food and anything tangible; he wet floors and beds and he hated sharing. In fairness to Matthew, the family had put undue emphasis on his looks without perhaps paying enough attention to his emotional place in the family. Whatever the causes, they could not cope with him. So, having just settled into a new routine with promises of special treats for his birthday and for Christmas, his first away from the hospital, Matthew was removed from the family. Fred and I still felt we would be able to cope. We hoped our children could cope, too.

After leaving his prospective adoptive home,

Matthew had temporarily gone back to live with Vivienne. She was in a difficult position: she had become a substitute mum for Matthew, taking him home at weekends and holidays, and caring for him as she would her own son. They loved each other very much. But she had her own life to lead and so could not take him in permanently. Instead, she was going to have to introduce us to Matthew, settle him in with us and leave him behind – it cannot have been easy for her. It was at her house, the day after we had visited Parents for Children in London, that we were to meet Matthew. Parents for Children had already vetted us, and they were well aware of our track record, having matched us with Sarah, which meant that the paperwork involved in Matthew's stay was fairly straightforward. And, so long as there were no hiccups during our meeting with Matthew, he would be allowed to live with us for three months.

I was scared about caring for Matthew – he was even more of a responsibility than many of our other kids, not least because his first taste of home life had failed. On the one hand we wanted to help him so much, and on the other we didn't want to get too involved with him because he would not be able to stay with us for more than three months. We were unsure of our own ability and afraid of letting him down, so causing more hurt to him. We wanted to make him feel relaxed and at home, but we also wanted him to feel happy about leaving our family for another one as soon as adoptive parents came forward or Matthew was found a place in a suitable foster home. It was going to be a tricky path to steer.

THE FAMILY

At least Fred and I know all about children with unusual problems. Apart from our own home-grown children who have no mental or physical handicap – Kevin, our eldest who is twenty-seven and in the Army; Stephen who is twenty-six; and Lorraine who has two children, four-year-old Zoe and two-year-old Jannine – we have an assortment of disabled children, some ˄ iopted and others permanently fostered, who will stay with us for the rest of our lives. The irony is that we decided to become short-term foster parents to babies and small children in 1961 when I was told that I was unlikely to be able to have children – I have a very rare blood group and Fred doesn't, so they thought I would miscarry. The very next year Kevin arrived, followed by the others. But by that time fostering had become part of our life and so we carried on.

When the youngest of our own children, Lorraine, was a toddler I could have gone back to work as a nurse, but I wanted to stay with her for those vital years before she went to school full-time. I wanted something more to do with my life, as well, and so I decided to try one step on from being a short-term foster parent. It had been heart-breaking to have to give back some of the children we had been caring for, so we decided to go ahead and adopt. Well I decided, because Fred was out at work each and every day and so, as he pointed out, most of the responsibility would fall on me. The bureaucratic procedures involved in adoption were complicated, long-drawn-out and off-putting. At that time, the local press was full of advertisements about fostering and adoption, and yet, as soon as you volunteered, you were put through a bewildering maze of interviews, police record checks, checks on references, checks on the physical and spiritual state of the home and interviews about family finances. Existing children, too, had to be interviewed by social workers. I was worried about our chances: our income was very low, we didn't own our house and we thought we would be considered too old. Also, we never went to church, although both Fred and I are believers. We have our own way of praying which does not involve going to church. We certainly believe in God but we do not feel the need to demonstrate our faith publicly, and we suspected that this might count against us. In short, we thought we wouldn't measure up to what they wanted although we knew we had a great deal to offer.

Almost in passing I mentioned to the social workers that I wouldn't mind caring for disabled or handicapped children because as a nurse I felt I would be able to manage. It was a decision that was to change our lives, and thanks to society's changing attitude to fostering and adoption, and to unusual and forward-looking agencies like Parents for Children, we were given a chance. Today, increasingly, the priority in the adoption system is to find a family for every child whatever their mental or physical problems – any child, any family so long as they are well-matched – rather than trying to create perfect families and then adding the children. It wasn't always so.

Five and a half months after our final interview with social workers, Ben arrived. He was five months old and weighed a pathetic five pounds. He had pulled through open-heart surgery, but the hospital didn't hold out much hope for this tiny baby. We were counselled and so were our own children; we were told that Ben was not feeding properly and that this might have something to do with his having been handled by so many different people – a new nurse on each shift – and so his chances might improve a little if he were cared for by the same people day-in, day-out. The counsellors explained to our children that Ben might not stay with them long because he might die and go to Jesus. So we wanted to make what we assumed would be the last few weeks of his life as happy and full of love as we could. The professionals were convinced he would die, but Ben had other ideas and today, although he isn't strong, he is alive and well thanks to a second major heart operation when he was five. Ben is twelve now with straw-coloured hair, large brown eyes, a wiry body and enough energy to supply the national grid. He keeps us on our toes: he has a mental handicap and he is hyperactive, so we have to have eyes in the backs of our heads to keep track of his activities: at the moment his favourite pastime is plumbing or anything that involves using tools. He is driving our plumber mad, and stays awake every night so that he won't miss our central heating workmen the following day.

Sarah was ten years old when she came to us in 1976. She is tall, slim and pretty, with a great mass of black Afro hair and large brown eyes. Today, if and when she is in a good mood, she is a friendly chatterbox with a large smile which can usually squeeze a reciprocal smile out of the gloomiest visitor. She arrived to stay with us after making headline news as a little girl who had suffered so many years of physical and mental abuse that she had been left in a coma. That day's news was the following day's fish-and-chip paper, but Sarah's problems couldn't be thrown away: she has brain damage, epilepsy, bad eyesight and she is severely emotionally disturbed. At first she could not walk very well. Now she has learned although her movements are still ungainly. But her determination has brought her through many problems. Sarah had learned about love: she had learned that love hurts because it gets rejected, and so to compensate she had wrapped herself up in her own cocoon and allowed herself love only for herself. No one else was allowed inside her world. By the time she arrived on our doorstep she had been taken into thirty-three sets of foster homes and residential institutions: only to be rejected and turned away when the going got tough. We nearly gave up there and then but somehow struggled on. We loved and hated, yes hated, and cried together.

Lorraine probably suffered the most with Sarah: she had always wanted a sister more than anything else, only to be told by Sarah, 'I hate you.' Sarah destroyed some of Lorraine's most prized possessions. There was her great grandmother's glass dressing-table set; her brand new, first-ever watch and some of her own drawings of which she was tremendously proud. It was as if anything Lorraine loved and cared for greatly became the things which Sarah had to break. Part of the problem was that all the treasures that Lorraine held dear were exactly the kind of thing which Sarah had never had but had always wanted. Lorraine was twelve years old but learned to forgive and love. She became a sister and a mother to Sarah, in the end, and it may have been all those ups and downs with Sarah that were to help us all when it came to coping with Matthew. We loved her till it hurt and couldn't let go even when she tried hard to make us reject her. It was a battle of wills, of emotions, of hard-learned lessons, but gradually we learned to understand and, for a while, at least, we managed to learn to live with each other. I suppose Fred and I and the family are just more stubborn than most.

Eddie, who is eighteen, has started a pop group with his brothers and sisters. As you can imagine, it is not well coordinated in sound or looks, but it is enterprising. He loves pop music and, like most boys of his age, he has recently discovered girls. He came to us four years ago, and he has cerebral palsy. He is a typical adolescent, happy one moment, down the next, childlike one day and above all that the next day. Luckily he has a sense of humour and he is always telling jokes. Here's his latest: 'What do you get when you cross a kangaroo with a sheep? A woolly jumper.' Boom, boom. At least that joke makes sense – most of them don't, but you have to laugh at the right time because he is trying so hard and, to him, it is the joke of the century.

Simon, who is twelve but with a mental age of between eighteen months and four years, will eat *anything*. Toy cars, plugs, shoe laces, worms – you name it, Simon will sample it; but, astonishingly, he has never been sick. He has a severe mental handicap, he has virtually no speech, he is still being toilet-trained and he dribbles. But he is loving, he smiles almost all the time, and he loves cuddles. He came to us four years ago wearing nappies day-in, day-out and now, thank heavens, he is daytime trained. Night-time training has proved more of a problem: he will proudly hand you his nappy in the morning, closely followed by his dry pyjamas and a demand for a sweet for having been a 'dry boy'. There are limits to what he can understand and so in the end he gets his sweet, but I sometimes wonder if he will ever get the message.

Then there's Lucy, a Down's syndrome six-year-old with an angelic face, a gorgeous smile and big blue eyes. No wonder she gets spoiled by visitors. So far

Lucy can say only a few baby words like 'Dad Dad' and 'Ma Ma' and 'Ta Ta', but she's learning. Her doctors thought she might never walk because, even by Down's syndrome standards, her leg muscles are exceptionally relaxed. But now she has to wear unladylike blue boots to give her greater support and, in January 1988, she took her first steps. Her crawling causes the most havoc. She is very inquisitive, and likes to investigate everything within her limited eyesight and crawling, reaching range. We kitted her up with glasses only to have them sat on, crawled on, and destroyed in every conceivable way, time and again. Luckily the optician is a patient man.

Finally there were the dogs. Gemma the Old English sheepdog, whose coat seemed to need more constant care and attention than Princess Diana's hair, was my twenty-fifth wedding anniversary present: I had always wanted a sheepdog. Then there was Boomer, the old black labrador cross who came from the RSPCA. She had been very cruelly treated. So at least Matthew would not feel lonely, at least he would have plenty of kids – and pets – to play with.

Our first meeting with Matthew, a week after the meeting with the social workers, began awkwardly. Matthew, still wary of 'families' after his one and only family experience, was tense and defensive, and we were nervous. Who wouldn't be nervous when meeting a new member of the family, however temporary that member was supposed to be? Vivienne was naturally sad about saying goodbye to Matthew, although she knew this was the best move for him in the long run because it was one step on the road to a permanent home.

Fred and I took most of the family to Vivienne's house to meet Matthew; that seemed only fair because all the family would be involved with him for the next three months. We fitted into the Hunter with difficulty: four children; Lorraine; Fred; me; a supply of crisps, drinks and sweets for the journey; nappies for Ben; a small model car and some Lego, prettily wrapped by Lorraine as a present for Matthew; and a written list of questions about Matthew for Vivienne. The questions were silly, practical things about him that natural parents would know and take for granted with their children: Was he scared of the dark? What food couldn't he eat? What were his favourite foods? Would he need a rubber sheet all the time? I wrote a list of the questions before we set out, otherwise I would never have remembered them all.

As Fred loaded up the car I wondered why it was that, on this of all days, the family was being even more chaotic and slow than normal. Coordinating a large family is slow at the best of times, but we tend to be even slower. Some of the children can wash and dress themselves while others need help, but although everyone knows his or her routine this was one of those days when amnesia and chaos ruled. Everyone was grumpy and no one could find shoes, socks, anything for the journey. If we didn't start soon we would never reach Vivienne's cottage in Surrey by lunch time, as agreed. It wasn't only the journey itself, which would have taken four hours in a normal car with a normal family, but our old banger didn't have much acceleration and we would have to make quite a few loo stops on the way. I was edgy – everyone was – and I began to feel like calling the whole thing off. Finally I screamed: 'Quiet. Or nobody goes anywhere.' It worked. Then I needed to calm myself, and I left the family to settle down while I had a cigarette and a coffee.

It was a chilly, dry morning with glorious blue skies, and the countryside was at that peak of autumn colour reached the week before the main leaf drop. We sang songs, we played 'I Spy' and we spotted cars.

24

Vivienne's neat white cottage was tucked away in a beautiful little lane a couple of miles from the nearest town centre, and thanks to Fred's sense of direction we found it first time. The cottage was old and picturesque, the kind which would not have looked out of place on a chocolate box. Vivienne was outside to meet us, waving and smiling. Matthew was nowhere to be seen.

Vivienne welcomed our motley crew and invited us in for some tea and biscuits while she left us for the garden where Matthew was playing. Inside the cottage, the whitewashed walls were decorated with corn dollies, the furniture was comfortable and the atmosphere homely, neat and cosy. I could understand why Matthew was so happy here. She returned with Matthew clinging to her, his arms wrapped about her neck, his legs about her waist. He looked more like a frightened monkey than a little boy. I remember thinking how small he looked, much, much smaller than in his photograph. Matthew didn't say anything, instead he just stared. He had been told what was going to happen but I do not think he understood what was going on. Our children were as bemused as we were. Sarah was too tongue-tied and shy to be able to do more than stare back at Matthew. Ben was more interested in Matthew's toys and went across to play with them. Lorraine and I wanted to have a closer look at Matthew, but this was hardly the time or place so, instead, we had to make smalltalk. Vivienne, still with her limpet-like human attachment, went into the kitchen where she tried to persuade Matthew to stop clinging and hand round the biscuits. He refused.

Fred, Vivienne and I started to talk about Matthew, while he, slowly and suspiciously, played with his Lego and model cars, although he would not leave Vivienne's side. Ben, ever friendly and smiling, went to join him. Matthew pushed a car to Ben, and gave us all a glance for the first time. Eventually he brought out some army badges he had collected free from petrol stations, but still he would not leave Vivienne until Fred told Matthew that he had been in the Army, once, and he would like to have a look at the badges. Breakthrough! at last. Matthew moved across to Fred, sat on his knee and told him about the badges. And gradually, as Matthew began to unwind, the rest of us followed suit. He invited us to the garden to see the chickens. He treated them like his pets and fed them every time he stayed with Vivienne. He even had names for them.

Matthew seemed pretty bright to me, but there was something about him that puzzled me, and I couldn't put my finger on it. Then it hit me. He had no expression. He didn't smile or scowl, his eyes didn't crinkle in amazement or pleasure – his eyes didn't blink – so it was impossible to see what he was feeling. The fact was that Matthew's face could not show expression in a way you or I might understand it – his strange slit mouth could not bend pleasingly at the corners, it couldn't do anything except open and shut, and his eyes did not close or blink because he had out-grown his grafted lids. The eyeballs moved but the flesh around them didn't. It is these tiny muscle changes which say so much in an ordinary face, but in Matthew's face there appeared to be a void. It was an odd feeling and it made me want to have a close exami-nation of his face. I remember feeling both repulsed and drawn to him. That is a common reaction to his appearance, although looking back at that first meeting I was surprised and ashamed that I was so taken aback by his looks. I am used to kids who dribble and hold their faces in peculiar ways, but Matthew's appearance was so strange that it took a while to get used to it. Matthew was used to over-curious stares and he hated them; so, as we were to discover, he kept his head lowered for as long as possible if there were strangers about. It took a lot of love and persuasion to get him to do otherwise, and to ignore the stares of strangers and look people straight in the eye, which usually makes them less curious and less inclined to gawp.

Vivienne explained some of Matthew's special needs, the most important of which was his skin-care routine. He has such dry skin that it cracks very easily, and if it were not well cared for it would bleed. Each day after tea Matthew is washed with a strange oatmeal and oil mixture because he is allergic to soap. It leaves the bath dirty and the boy clean – in theory, at least. That is followed by a rub all over with a type of cortisone cream. If his skin gets too dry at any other time of the day or night, he has to have a second dose of cream. She promised to show us in practice the following day when she would drive to our house to deliver Matthew and help him settle in. Vivienne was being brave. She did not want to let Matthew go, but she did want to give him a chance of having a happy family life which she, for practical reasons, was unable to provide. As we drove away at tea-time we looked back to see Vivienne and Matthew standing on the doorstep of the cottage waving us goodbye.

On the journey back Lorraine, practical as ever, asked where Matthew would go to school and what we would do if the other children started to make fun of him. I didn't have any answers. I hadn't thought that far ahead because it had been such a rush. It had been an emotionally draining day as first meetings always are, and all I wanted to do was get back, put all the children to bed and take my mind off Matthew's arrival the following morning by doing lots of odd jobs. I began by clearing parts of Ben's bedroom so that Matthew could move in. Fred and I scrunched up Ben's clothes, moved some of them elsewhere in the house and just prayed Matthew didn't have too many. We were a bit short of money so we certainly could not have afforded a new chest of drawers – Matthew and Ben would have to share. Matthew could use our son Steve's bed, and one of those big reddy-pink plastic bread crates for his toys. We fixed up a sixth hook in the bathroom for Matthew's flannel and got him his own toothpaste and soap: all children from institutions often find it hard to share anything at all, even tooth-paste. We try to give each child a space for him or herself. Later that night we asked each of the kids if they wanted to add one of their toys to Matthew's box. We always do this to help the children to learn to share. It helps the family settle down after a new arrival because then everyone is involved.

The children were exceptionally cooperative and quiet that night, and I got the feeling that they had formed an unspoken agreement to make Matthew's stay as happy as possible. They know what it is like to feel let down by one family and to have to face another and they also know how it feels to be handicapped, but somehow Matthew had appeared especially vulnerable and especially in need of love and security. The children went to bed with one or two sleepy questions about Matthew: What time will he arrive? How many toys has he got? Will he like the dogs? And, while the children slept, Lorraine sorted out some of her older brothers' toys and arranged them beside Matthew's bed.

BAD BEHAVIOUR

Twenty-four hours later Matthew was a fully-fledged, albeit temporary, member of the family. When he first arrived, he was still so shy that he refused to leave Vivienne's side, and so she agreed to stay with us until Matthew was in bed. As it turned out, she didn't need to because Matthew, egged on by Ben's infectious overexcitement, lost all inhibitions and became increasingly boisterous, rushing up and down the stairs and in and out of every room, exploring, shouting and letting rip.

After tea we managed to catch hold of this wild young tearaway long enough for Vivienne to show me how to bathe him and then rub the special cream all over his body. This was my first close look at Matthew. His legs carry scars from his thighs to his knees where skin was taken for his eyelids and for other surgery, the details of which we have never been able to discover. His toenails did not grow to the ends of his toes, so we would have to be careful about his shoes; he had webbed trigger fingers which could not straighten out; his eyes watered constantly because they did not have working tear ducts, and they had to be bathed very gently and regularly or they, too, bled. Vivienne explained that his eyes were especially vulnerable – even a bump on the back of the head could start a little bleeding from inside the sockets.

Soon after Matthew's bath Vivienne slipped quietly away. It was earlier than originally suggested but it was clear that Matthew was too preoccupied with his new home to feel nervous or homesick. Vivienne thoughtfully decided not to say goodbye to Matthew for fear of upsetting him. When Matthew realized she had gone there were only a few moments of gloom before he was whirled off into another game by the other children. For the time being he had too much to think about, too many new friends to get to know and too many new places to explore to dwell on what he had left behind.

Bedtime began well that night. Ben and Matthew went to bed with as much decorum as could be expected from two overexcited little boys. They seemed to get on well, and together they sorted out a bedtime story to listen to on the tape recorder. But when it came to saying goodnight I found myself hovering outside their bedroom door trying to decide how I would kiss Matthew. I was afraid or repulsed by the idea of kissing his face, and ashamed that I felt that way. I took a deep breath, breezed in and kissed Ben on the forehead. And did the same to Matthew while I wished him, 'Goodnight, God bless.' Matthew's skin is surprisingly soft and, although it looks odd, it feels like anyone else's. I was over one more hurdle.

A couple of hours later I did my second bedtime check on all the children. I always do that to make sure everyone is asleep. Matthew appeared to have relaxed during the day but I had a feeling that he might not be able to sleep in a strange house surrounded by strange people. I was a little more anxious than usual as I climbed the stairs to their bedrooms. A faint light from the hall shone across Matthew: his hands were folded across his chest, his eyes were wide open and staring straight up at the ceiling. I knelt beside him. 'What's wrong,' I whispered, 'can't you sleep?' But he made no reply. He didn't move. He didn't appear to be breathing. Shaking with sobs, I ran downstairs saying 'He's dead', over and over again. I dragged Fred to Matthew's bedside. Fred gently shook his shoulder and our latest addition sighed and turned over. 'You silly thing,' said Fred. 'They told us he sleeps with his eyes open and breathes very lightly.' I didn't know whether to laugh or cry.

Matthew stayed on a high for two days, during which time his good-humoured high spirits gave way to less attractive behaviour. The noise and speed with which he moved about our tiny house was enough in itself to create havoc. He quarrelled with the other children and disobeyed Fred and me. He would not let any of his new brothers and sisters borrow any of his toys, but if he wanted one of theirs he got it – or all hell would break loose. Matthew was strong-willed, bossy and territorial. He revelled in being the centre of attention and, while we were glad he had loosened up and we didn't want to spoil his fun, we decided we had to try to discipline him. We told him to stop going into our room or making too much noise downstairs in the sitting-room. It became clear that Matthew did not understand the word 'no'. A firm 'No' would bring on temper tantrums, with Matthew screaming and stamping his feet in the hope that we would give in. It might have worked at his hospital but it rarely did with us. He was very spiteful, demanding and greedy. If there were two or three cakes left by the end of tea Matthew would have to eat them all – even if he had already eaten huge amounts. He had to sit in front of the television and the fire regardless of who else was feeling cold or who else could not see the screen. He took great delight in destroying toys which belonged to the other children – he would pull the wheels off Ben's model cars or snap baby jigsaw puzzles in half.

He regularly borrowed toys from the other children but never let them play with his.

We try to avoid disciplining children by hitting or spanking them, and instead try to bring them round by reason. This usually works in the end. Sometimes it takes longer, sometimes shorter than normal, but it requires a great deal of patience. Luckily our own children have seen it all before – they know that, eventually, there will be peace and harmony, but it is not easy to put up with the kind of behaviour Matthew was displaying. It was typical of many of the institutionalized children we have looked after over the years. They have had to carve out their own, tiny, precious piece of safe space, they have had to look after themselves against the sometimes impersonal institution that has cared for their physical needs alone and so, naturally, they become grasping and greedy, and virtually unable to share anything. Gradually, as they learn that things they lend really do come back, and that in order to borrow it is only fair to lend toys as well, their trust and love grow and they can begin to relax. It takes a lot of explaining and love, and it takes tolerant children, but we have rarely failed. And so these were the rules we applied to Matthew: explaining why he should or should not do something, and frequently having to stand over him until he had done what was asked of him and made some grudging attempt to apologize if he had hurt any of the children.

At least most of his behaviour stemmed from having lived so long in institutions rather than from bloody-mindedness. Matthew refused to bother to turn off lights, he left the front and back doors open so we were heating all the street, and, when we explained that if he did these things we would not be able to pay the electricity and gas bills, Matthew suggested that we go down to the bank and get some more money. He had no conception of the idea of a limited supply of money, money that has to be earned before it can be spent; he didn't know you had to put money into a bank before you can take it out. We had a lot of explaining to do, a lot of re-educating to free him from his 'institutional' habits. For instance, time, or how to use his own time, meant nothing to Matthew. His days revolved around breakfast, lunch, tea and supper. He used to wait downstairs in the mornings asking when the breakfast trolley would arrive. If I told him we would be going shopping at ten o'clock, so he had better be ready, then he would have no idea what I meant: for him the day was mapped out by meals, not minutes. For the first time in his life his routine of activities and outings was not being planned and organized for him.

He was very unworldly in many ways. Once he nearly drove me to distraction when we were trying to get ready to visit a friend: I told him to put on his shoes. Which shoes? What colour? Why should I wear those ones? Where are they? Why don't you put them on me? Followed by the same lethargy and set of questions when I told him to put on his coat, jumper, gloves and hat. Finally I lost my temper and shouted, 'For God's sake, pull your socks up, Matthew.' So he did just that. Through helpless laughter I had to tell him what I meant. Just the same thing happened when we were driving to Dover with a friend. The friend stopped the car and said he was going to see a man about a dog. Matthew was beside himself with excitement: What kind of dog was it going to be? Was it a puppy or a big dog? He was crestfallen to find out that our friend had simply been going to the toilet.

There were times, though, when I was not so amused by Matthew's antics. Once I discovered him pulling faces at Ben to frighten him into doing what he wanted. He was telling Ben he had to love him, and not his mum and dad. He was telling Ben he had to do

33

everything he wanted him to do. Matthew tried this trick on all the children and for a while ruled them like a little tyrant, bullying them to do his every whim. It was difficult not to be angry, but after lots of cuddles and explanations for them all, after showing Matthew that Sarah or Eddie or Ben could love lots of people and still have plenty of love for him, he calmed down. During the first month I lost my temper once or twice over Matthew's intransigence and bullying. I never hit or spanked him – we rarely do – but once when I shouted at him we had tears followed by, 'Well, you're not my real mum anyway. I'm going back to Vivienne.' I was very glad he didn't.

After the first week, when I hoped he would begin to settle, Matthew seemed especially agitated about something. What was wrong? Why, he asked, were Fred and I still on duty? When was there going to be a staff change and who was going to take our place? He also complained about the dust and asked what day the cleaner came. Family life was beyond anything he knew or understood. Mind you, our family life cannot really be described as run-of-the-mill. Apart from the fact that we are a mixed bunch, we have many close friends and neighbours who treat our home like theirs – they are always popping round to say hello or lend a hand. And so any new addition becomes a matter of concern for them. We had given pictures of Matthew to the 'network' of close friends at that time so that they and their children could get used to his appearance before they met him. Gradually they came round to be introduced to him. At first almost everyone was taken aback by his looks, but that soon changed as the real Matthew came through. Slowly but surely Matthew was becoming one of the family. As he did, the trust between him and the rest of us grew and with it love and a sort of intermittent peace.

A more attractive side of Matthew's personality

34

began to peep through the bullying and bad behaviour. I first noticed it when Ben, Matthew's room-mate, had one of his vomiting fits. Ben often gets breathless and tired, but if he overdoes things he can become quite sick. The first time this happened after Matthew had moved in, I found Matthew crouching beside Ben's bed sounding very upset: 'Is he going to be all right?' he asked me over and over again. It was Matthew who went off for a sick bowl and a damp flannel to cool Ben's forehead, and it was Matthew who stayed at Ben's bedside throughout the illness. He went back to bullying Ben as soon as he was up and about, but at least now it was clear that Matthew had a reservoir of good nature just waiting to be tapped.

The transformation was slow but wonderful to watch: day by day Matthew changed from a wild little boy, aggressively defending himself and his territory, to a more caring, outgoing child. However corny it may sound, I feel strongly that although God did not give Matthew a complete face He gave him something far greater.

BEDLAM

There is one golden rule in the Learoyd household: things never go according to plan, and so chaos is an integral part of the routine. Each child has his or her special way of wrecking any systematic timetable I try to organize. Take Ben, for instance. He goes through phases of flushing everything down the lavatory. Once, I found him standing over the pan watching with delight as the water gushed over the side of the pan. 'Ben good boy, mummy,' he said as he tried to flush his trousers away. This is a fairly regular event in family life, and provides local plumbers with plenty of work. Ben has been known to create good business for local Sunday-opening supermarkets, too: he has twice fed the Sunday joint to the dogs. These are just a couple of examples of the way our household is more of a shambles than most. It must have been quite a change for Matthew after life in a well-ordered long-stay hospital.

We have an unusual family and therefore we have unusual ways of organizing family life, and we have to allow ourselves at least twice as much time as ordinary households for even the most mundane tasks like getting dressed. That means we have to get up earlier than most. Matthew, Eddie and Ben dress themselves, usually; Simon and Lucy have to be helped. Sarah, too, needed occasional assistance. Fred and I work a relay system each morning. Whoever gets up first makes the breakfast and the tea while the other helps dress the children. Everything has to be done in order, and the dressing has to be supervised, each item of clothing being handed out in order. Otherwise the underpants might go on over the trousers!

I do most of the cooking and cleaning, and in the old days before we had a dishwasher everyone used to help with the washing-up. Thanks to plastic cups, plates and cutlery, the children took it in turns to wash up without costing us a fortune in breakages. Now Matthew is the only one involved in the washing-up – he is the only one allowed to fill the dishwasher. The children always make their beds – well, they try to – and as soon as they go off to school, Fred and I pop upstairs and do them properly. Fred and I have learned to do several things at the same time, like watching the television while we are dressing or undressing the children, helping them with their homework, or playing with them. We, the family, can do anything just so long as we have enough time.

Time – and patience. Today we have a larger house than the one in Aylesham, so I have one room which is just for me – no one else is allowed in it, and it is called my sanity room. It's my bolt hole, my escape-hatch when life is madder than usual. There I sometimes sit and daydream about what I would be if I weren't who I am. I think I would be a designer, a clothes designer. I love classic designs or very way-out clothes like kaftans – the kind of thing I could never wear. My sanity room is the nearest I get to fulfilling my dreams, because I keep my sewing machine there and make clothes for the children. For instance, boys who use wheelchairs need much higher-cut trousers than normal because their trousers tend to work their way down very easily. And, depending on the child's handicap, I put zippers, hooks or buttons in unusual places on the clothes or I replace fasteners altogether with Velcro to make dressing and undressing easier. If I have time I make clothes for other disabled children, too, but mostly it's just for our own. I used to make trousers for Fred but now he's so big that it's cheaper to buy them! I also make soft toys – dolls and cuddly creatures – from bits of old curtains, fabric oddments from friends, anything. I give them to the children or I sell them to make a little extra cash, which is always in short supply. Fred gets away from it all by reading adventure and war stories or by playing darts. He's a good darts player, and has just started in two local teams. It gets him out of the house and it's a little less energetic than the football and cricket he used to play.

Our routine, in so far as we can ever have one, was increasingly unsettled by Matthew's arrival. Usually it works the other way round: as a child settles down, so our 'routine' gets back to normal. The problem was that after the first few weeks, when Matthew had begun to get used to us and to trust us, he began to get bored. He took to following me around the house like a shadow; if I stepped back suddenly, I would tread on Matthew. And every hour or so he would say he couldn't think of anything to do, so could I think up a game? He missed being with lots of other children at the hospital, and he missed our own children when they went to school, so Fred and I had to spend lots of extra time and effort entertaining him, playing with him and taking him on car trips. It was tough for him. Every day the rest of the family would troop off to their special school, leaving him behind. And when they returned they were sometimes too sleepy to want to play with him. The answer was clear: Matthew would have to go to school, even though he was staying with us for such a short time.

From what little we had been told about Matthew's mental development, and from what we had learned in our first couple of days with him, Fred and I decided that he was probably an exceptionally bright boy. He had a well-developed imagination which took off when he played with his Lego and built things quite unlike anything in the manufacturers' handbooks. Sometimes, if we could get him to sit still for long enough, he would dream up ideas like a design for a spaceship and then draw it with every detail. He would paint pictures of the inside and outside, and then make up adventure stories about going up in the spaceship. He also asked questions constantly, on top of the irritating 'where are my socks?'-type demands which all the children make when they start with us. He would ask Fred about car engines and, whenever the old banger needed any work, Matthew would be out there 'helping' Fred; as long as he could hold a spanner and get a bit oily I don't think he minded how much tinkering he actually did with the engine. He would ask me about cooking, and help me prepare some of our meals. He has become an accomplished pastry cook, making all sorts of delicacies including marble cake, fruitcakes and pizzas. Even our neighbours came in for cross-questioning about anything and everything they were doing. He was so nosy and inquisitive about the world that we thought: 'At last, we've got a bright one.'

Well, Matthew is bright, practical, quick and highly articulate, but academically he will never break any records. And when he first arrived he could not read or write very well because he had taken so much time off for his dozen or so operations. He had reached the educational standard of a five-year-old, and so it was important that we get him into a school, even if it was only for a month or so. At least he would catch up a little.

Our daughter Lorraine had gone to the local village school, Aylesham Junior, which was only ten minutes away. It was a friendly neighbourhood school of about 700 children. Just what Matthew needed. But would the headmaster, Mr Whitting, be prepared to take Matthew on – and what would the other children make of Matthew? And how would he cope with them? I phoned Mr Whitting and went to see him the following day. I made my way across the grass playing-field and the playground into the one-storey building to Mr Whitting's study. He has a reputation for being good with all kinds of children, and sure enough he agreed to take Matthew in on a trial basis. By the end of that meeting, Mr Whitting had already thought of an ingenious way to make Matthew's first few days at the school as easy as possible. He asked if he could keep the large picture of Matthew I had taken with me to the school, and during assembly the following morning he held it up for everyone to see, explained Matthew's problem, announced when he would arrive, and passed the photograph round to all the children. Later that day we brought Matthew in on the pretext of showing him around the school; but it was really to show him to the children so that they could make their comments and ask their teachers about him before his arrival.

There was no uniform to buy, and formal preparations were few. Matthew would be on trial to see how he fitted in. To our relief it was clear from the first week that Matthew and his school were going to get along just fine. He made friends quickly and after the first couple of weeks went to tea with his school friends as often as he brought them back to tea with us. We always seem to have so many people around the house that a few extra never make much difference. The teachers were understanding and encouraging, although they pointed out that Matthew was never likely to become a scholar. He learned to read slowly and even then showed only minimal interest in the three 'R's. Art was probably his main strength, and a few days after starting at Aylesham Junior he returned home, triumphant, with his first art-class picture as a present for us. It was a large, brightly-coloured painting of our house, with me, Fred and all his brothers and sisters standing outside. He was very excited about it, and we were proud of his work, although I was a little surprised that he had painted me as a redhead when mousy blonde is my natural colour!

The oddest thing about those first days was the way in which the older, rougher boys were the ones who cared for Matthew. They took him under their wing and protected him from the stares of the younger children. The tiny children were too scared to look at Matthew to begin with, and that was perhaps the most difficult part of his new school life. They soon got used to him, though, and when they saw him playing, coughing, sneezing and even getting into trouble with the teacher just like everyone else, Matthew was soon completely accepted, and his looks were forgotten and ignored.

Just as Matthew was settling down to his new life there came news of another upheaval: the council wrote to say that they had found a new, larger house for our growing family. We had forgotten we were on their list for a bigger house, so the news came as a shock. They had found us a five-bedroomed, pebble-dashed house in Walmer near Deal, which is on the Kentish coast. It was seventeen miles away from Aylesham and, although it sounded like a wonderful opportunity to spread ourselves after our cramped surroundings, I knew I would miss all our friends very much. And what about Matthew, who had just started school. He needed security and permanence. There was nothing for it. We would have to accept this offer, but I did not look forward to moving.

They say that moving house is one of the most stressful things you can do. I can now vouch for that. It was a terrible wrench to have to uproot the entire family. And there were so many people to tell, from the Gas Board to distant relatives; none of the curtains fitted the new house; we didn't have enough furniture; we didn't have enough carpet – and we had two weeks to sort everything out. The task I most dreaded was packing the children's toys: what if some prized possession went missing during the move? The already upset child would spend weeks in mourning. As always our friends rallied and helped us with the packing, cleaning and tidying. Jean and Richard Norton threw themselves into helping us. The Nortons are in their forties. Jean is short and dark with a pretty, rounded figure, short hair and bundles of energy. She is always on the go, looking after her children and helping with everyone else's. Richard is much quieter than Jean; he is a tall, well-built man who works for the Post Office and spends his spare time gardening. He grows all their fruit and vegetables in no more than about a third of an acre. They are foster parents who, like us, will take on children with problems. We met each other through regular local foster parent groups, where we would get together to discuss, and solve, problems. At that time the Nortons were living in Dover, which is about twenty miles from Aylesham, and as soon as they heard we were moving Jean offered to help me clean up the new house.

The house was a tip. And it was very, very cold. Anyway, we filled sack after sack with rubbish from all the rooms and from under the floorboards. The stash under the floorboards was an education – it included magazines which would, I think, have interested the police and customs and excise people! We cleaned and scrubbed every inch of the three-storey house, and we decorated the top two rooms so that the boys could take one room and the girls the other until the rest of the house had been decorated. The décor had to be seen to be believed. I've never before seen wallpaper attached to the walls by drawing pins! And all the painted walls were a different colour – bright blue or red or yellow.

By the end of one week, two bedrooms, the living-room and the kitchen were habitable and, above all, the house was clean, so we could move in. But it was still freezing because there was no central heating. On moving day, Jean and Richard looked after the children while we directed the removals men and sorted out the most important packing cases. As soon as we arrived at the new house, Fred lit a coal fire in the living-room so that at least one room would be warm. Or that was the plan, anyway. But in fact on that day there were blizzard conditions, and, as every piece of furniture was carried in, a biting wind howled through the house and large swirls of snow landed inside. I had put on my warmest clothes. Layer upon layer of socks and jumpers and vests, but I was still so cold that I cried. As the last removals man left, and as the snow mounted in drifts outside our new front door, Fred went to buy us some fish and chips, our first hot food all day. We made one last trip back to Aylesham that night to say goodbye to all our friends and to kind Mr Whitting, the headmaster, who still carries Matthew's picture in his breast pocket. Then we returned to spend our first night in our new home. The house was still cold, but it had a good atmosphere and we knew we were going to be happy.

MATTHEW FOR EVER

The new house was near enough to the old one to enable the same group of social workers to visit the children, so at least that was one less disruption to our so-called routine. Every foster child has to have regular visits from his or her social worker – that is the law – and our children were no exception. Even Matthew, who was due to be with us for only three months, had his own social worker who used to come once a month to see if he was all right and if he was happy with the family. The usual time between visits, which normally last for a couple of hours, is six to eight weeks, but the frequency varies according to the age of the child and the reason that he or she is being fostered.

When one child's social worker arrives, he or she usually tries to have a chat with the other children to get a picture of the family and how his or her charge fits in. They often end up playing games in the sitting-room. It was during one of these visits that we learned no one had come forward to adopt Matthew. It was nearly three months since Matthew had joined us and, although that was only the provisional time limit of his stay (there are no hard-and-fast rules about bridging stays because the fortunes of children and families are never predictable), we had organized family life around a three-month time space for Matthew's stay.

Three days after that news came the letter from our son Steve saying he was going to return home, and so, finally, we were forced into making a firm decision about Matthew. If Matthew stayed Steve wouldn't have a bed.

We loved Matthew very much, even though he still threw the odd tantrum, and he loved us. Matthew was part of our family now and had fitted in far better than I had dared hope in the first few weeks of his stay. Apart from learning and sticking to the unwritten rules of the Learoyd household, he had started to contribute to family life: he was very fond of his room-mate, Ben, and took especial protective care of him. But he was also increasingly thoughtful and kind to the other children, helping them on with overcoats and shoes when we were busy and, from time to time, helping us with a few household chores.

There was no doubt that we all loved him and therefore it was natural that we should at least consider the idea of keeping him on a longer-term basis. But his problems were so great that we had to think carefully about whether or not we were the right people to help him and about whether we were going to be able to manage. In some respects we felt he might be better off in a smaller family than ours where he would get more attention. We knew the real Matthew, but the world outside still focused on his grotesque looks. How would he cope when girls rejected him? Would he get a job? Would he become emotionally unstable as he reached adolescence? On the other hand, the rest of the family had grown to love him and the uncertainty over his future was not contributing to a stable family life. Ben in particular was very fond of Matthew and sometimes became angry when we reminded him that Matthew would not always live with us.

In practical terms, looking after Matthew long-term would present many problems and so, before we all got too fond of each other, we decided to take a deep breath, tell Matthew about Steve's homecoming and remind him that he would soon have to move on to another, more permanent home. And that was when, as I've already said, Matthew informed us in no uncertain terms that we could adopt him, and that he would be staying.

It was the winter of 1982-83, and the morning after Matthew had put us right about our mutual future. Fred and I had talked about Matthew's future until we were blue in the face. Finally, we reached our decision and contacted his social workers to tell them that we wanted to look after Matthew on a more long-term basis. We told them that we might even want to adopt him. They suggested that we keep Matthew as a permanent foster child and that, later, if we still felt we had made the right decision, we could adopt him. There would be a little paperwork to complete but, apart from that, the decision had been made. As a result of that telephone call we had acquired one more very special child.

Matthew was over the moon. I had never seen him so excited and he tore round the house to give everyone the news. They took it in their stride, because they had always tried to ignore Matthew's temporary status: as far as they were concerned he was already part of the family for keeps and his legal position with us made little difference to them. We didn't have any particular celebration that day – just a big happy family tea, although perhaps it was a little noisier and a little more fun than usual.

We knew right away that we had made a good decision, and it made a lovely start to our new life in our new home. It was a good omen. The family took to Deal and the adjoining town of Walmer straight away, although Walmer took rather longer to warm to us. I remember seeing net curtains twitching wildly as our motley crew pulled up for the first few times. I don't blame them – we look pretty strange. The children arrived a couple of days after us, having spent the few days on either side of moving day with our friends, Jean and Richard Norton. As soon as they arrived at their new home we set off to explore the town. It is picturesque. The old town of narrow, twisting streets runs parallel to a pebble beach down to the sea, where one or two fishing fleets still operate. The fishermen pull their boats up on to the beach and sell fresh fish there and then. Even at that time of year it looked beautiful, with the great grey waves crashing on to the pebbles. But Walmer and Deal are more than picture-postcard scenes – between them they have most of the major high-street names, so shopping was going to be easy.

We explored the area, crunched along the beach, and turned the corner to see a magical scene – the children could hardly believe their eyes. There, in the distance on the edge of the sea, stood a castle just waiting to be explored. It was getting dark, so that treat would have to wait for another day. The children found another castle further on down the beach at Walmer where, it is rumoured, the Queen Mother stays fairly regularly, as Lord Warden of the Cinque Ports. Between the two castles, which are about one and a half miles apart, there was a lifeboat surrounded by lots of smaller boats and dinghies. Inland, and again only walking distance from our street, there were woods and open fields. There was so much to see, so much for the children to do. I was delighted – this was going to be an excellent area in which to live.

A couple of weeks after we had moved into Walmer it was Christmas Day. The house was decorated and we set up a ceiling-high Christmas tree in the sitting-room. The children were so excited that, as always, they got up at about four o'clock to open their pillow-

cases full of toys. Fred and I had hardly shut our eyes
after putting out the pillowcases and going to bed
before we heard the first pair of bare feet scuffling
down the stairs to find out if Father Christmas had
been. This was followed by loud stage whispers of
'He's been', which signalled the start of the stampede
downstairs in pyjamas and dressing-gowns to rip open
all the presents. Eventually the shouts of 'Look at this'
and 'What have you got?' were too loud to sleep
through, so Fred and I went downstairs to wade
through the wrapping paper and make some tea.
There is no way we would have got them to table
when breakfast time came, so we just dished up the
cereal and handed round the bowls to the children
where they sat. After coaxing them away from their
new-found toys, we washed and dressed them, and
Fred brought them back down to the sitting-room to let
them play with their toys and watch the television. I
retreated to the kitchen to start making Christmas
lunch – turkey, Christmas pudding and all the
trimmings – most of which I had managed to prepare
on Christmas Eve.

Grandma, my mother who is sixty-six and lives in
Ramsgate, joined us for Christmas lunch as she always
does. My mother and I are like chalk and cheese. She
was a nurse, an assistant anaesthetist, and was and
still is a local councillor as well as a member of many
committees, from trades unions to the local area health
authority. I can remember as a child sitting in various
committee rooms listening to council officials and
councillors carry out their work with the help of my
mother. That was at a time when it was more unusual
to have a working mum, and it gave me a chance to
decide for myself whether to have a career, a family or
both. I think she would like me to have had more of a
career, but I have made my family my career and
wouldn't have it any other way. There was a quick

flurry before she arrived while Fred and I decorated the table with Father Christmas serviettes and a centre-piece made by one of the children at school with holly, glitter, baubles and a central candle. Each place-setting had a cracker and a glass – a great honour for the children who normally drink out of plastic cups – to toast Happy Christmas in Coke or lemonade. The grown-ups drank table wine.

After lunch, the washing-up and the Queen's speech the children gave us our presents. Sometimes the gifts are things they have made at school, like pictures or clay models or decorations based on washing-up liquid bottles. Otherwise the children will save their pocket money for weeks and weeks to buy us and each other presents. Just before Christmas Fred takes the children into town to buy presents for me, and then I do the same for them to buy presents for him. They usually choose weird and wonderful things for us: a box of matches because we smoke, or a candle in case the lights go out. But each gift is so magnifi-cently wrapped it looks as if it could contain the crown jewels. No one gets left out in our house and the dogs would always do particularly well on doggy choc drops at Christmas.

The dogs and the children spent the rest of the day grinding half-eaten sweets, nuts and broken toys into the carpets, while we collapsed in front of the fire. The children were half playing with their new toys, half watching the television, but I noticed that Matthew was getting grumpy. I thought he was tired and over-excited, until he came across and asked, 'When are they coming?' 'Who?' I asked. 'Them,' he said. I didn't understand what he meant at first. But then I remembered that in hospital after Christmas lunch the entertainers arrive: a puppet show, clowns and Father Christmas, amongst others. This was Matthew's first Christmas outside an institution and he wasn't about to let standards falter. He was not impressed with our explanation and a tantrum ensued, although not as extreme as the ones he used to have when he first arrived. But it reminded us how much we assumed he knew and how much learning he still had to do.

Christmas is always a family time, but on Boxing Day friends and neighbours began to call round for a drink and to give us our presents. It was lovely to see all our old friends and neighbours from Aylesham, but just as good to find that a lot of our new neighbours were popping round to say hello and to make sure we'd had a happy first Christmas in our new home.

With Christmas and the move behind us we had time once more to focus on Matthew, or, to be more precise, on Matthew's education. Now that he was going to be with us permanently we had to find him a new school. The other children continued to go to their special school, they just had to be taken by a different bus. The problem was that the academic year had begun and most of the schools in the area were full. We were given a list of local schools to try, and the first was a small Roman Catholic school. We are not Catholic and Matthew wasn't even christened, but it has such a good reputation I decided to try it.

This time I took Matthew with me. I felt at ease with Mr Seller, the headmaster, as soon as we were introduced: he is a gentle, pleasant man, with wavy greying hair, glasses and a soft voice. He was interested in Matthew and agreed to take him for a trial period – one term. Funnily enough, I don't think he was concerned about Matthew's appearance. His main worry seemed to be that he had no special facilities for non-Catholics, so Matthew would have to attend the daily lesson on religion. We weren't in the least bothered – it would give Matthew a chance to widen his outlook. Mr Seller used the same pattern to introduce Matthew as had been used at his last school –

showing the children a large picture of Matthew beforehand – and once again the method worked well. The children got all their questions and most of their shock out of the way before Matthew arrived.

If anything, Matthew settled in rather too well. It was not long before he had begun a little ring-leading on the side, a secret we discovered at a parents meeting when we overheard one or two conversations about Matthew. Parents referred to him in hushed tones as the school's mischief-maker, although I'm glad to say he was not known as a bully. He regularly got into fights, and attracted tellings-off for talking in class. But if he was naughty he was also popular and, even if he did irritate the teachers a little some of the time, he was at least being treated – and he was behaving – like any little boy, which is what he wanted and we wanted.

JUDGEMENT DAY

We had adopted three children without any problems and yet when it came to adopting Matthew, on 26 July, 1985, I found myself shaking from head to foot, worried the judge would say 'No'. The judge was much more relaxed than we were. Matthew's lips always go white when he is nervous. They were very white, and he was fidgeting, which is another give-away about how worried he is feeling, however nonchalant he is pretending to be. It was only when he got to the court that he began to get nervous; until then he had accepted everything as only Matthew can. That morning he dressed in his school uniform – navy blue blazer with the school badge, pale blue shirt, navy trousers and a navy and pale blue striped tie – as if it were a normal school day.

We had arrived early at the Town Hall in Dover, which houses the law courts, and climbed the stone steps through the main entrance to a high-roofed hall in which daggers, spears, helmets and shields decorate the walls. The place was swarming with people who seemed to know exactly what they were doing and where they were going. We asked one of the many men in gowns to show us where our court was.

In fact, Matthew's adoption was to take place in a

small, informal anteroom off the main court, and there we – Fred, me, Ben, Eddie and Lorraine – met Matthew's headmaster Mr Seller and the school secretary Mrs Settle, who had been invited simply because Matthew liked them both so much. This courtroom scene was the culmination of over a year's work by social workers, court officials and us to make sure that adoption was the right route for all concerned. An official, appointed by the court to look after Matthew's best interests, had visited him three times to make sure he understood the importance of the decision he was making and to make sure this was something he genuinely wanted. The court official arrived and so did Matthew's social worker Hadi Argent, who brought with her all his records so that they could be altered to his new name: Matthew because that was his given name; Patrick after Patrick Seller, his headmaster, for whom he had the greatest respect; Mark after a close school friend. He had told us the names he wanted while we were washing-up one evening. We try never to make a big fuss over anything. We had reminded Matthew that he could have some new names if he wanted so he might like to think about it, and those were the names he picked.

Like every judge involved in adoption, this one went out of his way to make the proceedings informal so that Matthew would not feel intimidated. He shook hands with us, settled us into battered leather seats around his chambers, explained simply but thoroughly what was involved in adoption, and then asked us a series of questions: Did we all understand what was involved? Did we understand the responsibilities involved? Were we quite sure? Then he took Matthew aside and quietly asked him about his mum and dad, and brothers and sisters. He wanted to know if Matthew was happy with us, he wanted to know if Matthew was sure he wanted to stay with us for ever.

Finally, he asked Matthew directly if he was happy and if he wanted to be adopted. Matthew said he did. The judge moved back to his desk and opened Matthew's file of social workers' reports. He seemed to ponder over those papers for a lifetime, but at last he asked Matthew what names he wanted. 'Matthew Patrick Mark'.

Finally the adoption order could take place. Matthew was *our son*, and as the last of the paperwork was sorted out the judge let Ben and Matthew dress up in his magnificent crimson, fur-edged robes and his wig. Although he was wearing one, he had a large box full of wigs beside his desk. While they played he told them about his grandchildren. As we were leaving with our new son, we were called back by an usher. My stomach churned – had the authorities changed their mind? No, the judge had been so busy entertaining Ben and Matthew that he had forgotten to sign the papers!

Our convoy of cars made its way back from Dover to our house and to a buffet with a square white cake decorated with blue icing which read 'Congratulations, Matthew, on your adoption'. We toasted each other with wine while the boys stuck to fizzy drinks. At the end of the meal, each of the guests received a bouquet of chrysanthemums and carnations from Matthew as a thank you for their part in his day. Matthew and I thought it a good idea to give everyone a special reminder. The following day Matthew returned to school to tell his class about his new beginning.

But Matthew's school friends were even more interested in his second new beginning. Matthew had decided that he wanted to become a Catholic. It happened slowly and gradually. His desire to become a Catholic never faltered but grew steadily, unlike some of his other ambitions – from soldiering to lorry-driving – which changed by the week. It became clear that this was more than a passing craze or phase. Quite soon after he had joined St Mary's School, he announced that he loved Catholic services and that he wanted to be christened. We felt that this was such an important commitment that we stalled. Also, we felt we couldn't give a definite yes or no while there was still a chance he would leave us for another family. Now that he was adopted, and a year had passed during which his activities with the Church had grown consistently, we began to take his ambition more seriously. As I have said, both Fred and I believe in God and, although the faith that Matthew had chosen was not one we followed, we were not going to stand in his way. Catholicism was clearly something that mattered a great deal to him, it was his decision and we could respect that so long as we felt sure he understood what an important decision it was.

Through Matthew we met Joyce Deadman, who was in charge of the vestments in the chapel beside Matthew's school, and it was through Joyce that we discovered that Matthew had unwittingly broken all the rules. He was an altar server despite the fact that he was a non-Catholic. During his duties as an altar server he had even been presented to Archbishop Henderson and Bishop John Dukes from the diocese of Southwark while the two men were visiting St Mary's. The local papers were at the presentation and that week published pictures of Matthew, the Archbishop and the Bishop. It was probably the first time Matthew had received any Press attention but, instead of being pleased, he took one look at the paper and pushed it to one side. 'I look like a black blob,' he said, and complained that the black and white paper clearly wasn't used to reproducing pictures of coloured people.

Matthew had learned a lot about Catholicism and so he had much to teach us. Since we are non-practising

Church of England, the Catholic traditions and services meant nothing to us, and neither Fred nor I go to church unless to a funeral, a christening or a wedding; we prefer to worship God in our own way. What Matthew could not explain was filled in by Joyce, and so after every service I would ring her to find out what had happened and what part, if any, Matthew had played. We began to realize just how important Catholicism was to Matthew when he went to Lourdes in France, where he helped to serve at the altar in the Grotto of St Bernadette. One of the photographs of Matthew which hangs on our sitting-room wall shows him, dressed in red and white vestments, looking more angelic than I ever thought possible – and I can't help feeling that the vestments are covering dirty knees! Knowing Matthew he would have had a game of football before dressing, and probably wouldn't have washed. His answer, when caught, is that his knees won't show anyway because they are under his trousers. Typical boy.

All the pupils at Matthew's school went to Mass in the chapel beside the school building at least once a week, as well as attending regular special services. Once Matthew came home bursting with the news that he had been to a funeral as an altar boy. I was a little shocked because I felt it might have disturbed him. I asked him whose funeral it was, and was taken aback by his reply: 'I don't know. He was in a box.' It was clear that the experience had not upset him and that, whatever happened, Matthew was determined to demonstrate his faith and be christened.

Matthew's christening arrangements began a month or so after his adoption. It is a long process, and rightly so. After all, it is such a commitment on both sides that everyone involved has to be very sure it will work. Joyce Deadman and Matthew's priest, Father Parkinson, came to tea at our house to explain what was involved. Father Parkinson was the first Catholic priest we had met, and he was not how I had imagined a priest to be: I think I had expected him to be pious and aloof – he wasn't. He was gentle and great fun, although he was not soft; he had that understated air of authority which is sometimes displayed by one or two teachers at parent-teacher evenings, or by experienced, well-respected consultants. As he explained what would happen in the service, he dragged on cigarettes and swigged sugar-laden tea – both commodities are forbidden because he has a heart problem, but that didn't seem to stop him.

Matthew chose Joyce Deadman as one of his god-parents, and asked Rita Burrows to be the other. Joyce had become a close family friend, and since Matthew had started school in Walmer she had been in regular contact with us to keep us up to date with his latest antics. She has a broad Scottish accent which Matthew loves to imitate. Once, she got cross with him and shouted, 'I'll box your ears', to which he replied, 'But I haven't got any'. And no one could argue with that. Rita is the mother of Matthew's best friend, Darren, who had invited Matthew home to tea soon after he had joined the school. Rita brought Matthew home that evening, stayed and talked. Over the next year or so she and her husband, Brian, became as close to Fred and me as Matthew became to Darren and his brother and sister, Paul and Hayley, who all went to school together. Rita and Brian are a second mum and dad to Matthew. He has come to use their house as his own. Brian is as tall as Rita is short, and they both have boundless energy, which is a good thing when it comes to coping with all the boys. Once Rita told the boys they would have to stop breakdancing because they were wearing out her carpets. Two days later she arrived back to find Darren, Paul and Matthew standing in the sitting-room, holding a roll of lino:

they had bought it with their pocket money to protect the carpets from their dancing.

Rita is an absolute lunatic. She is the sort of person who would throw off her shoes and start break-dancing with the kids if she actually saw them doing it. She works part-time at Marks and Spencer but she always puts her children – and Matthew for that matter – first. She treats Matthew as one of her own, and never lets him get away with anything. When she first knew Matthew she told him to help with the washing-up after tea; he replied that he couldn't because he was allergic to water. Well, it was a nice try but Rita saw through it straight away. Matthew did the washing-up! And precisely because she treated him like a son, like one of her own family, he felt it appropriate that she should be his godparent.

The selection of godparents was entirely Matthew's although Fred and I discussed the final choice at length with him because there were so many to choose from, so many people who were special to Matthew and who loved him as well as their own children. When we had drawn up a short list of possible godparents I phoned them to check if they would be willing to take on the responsibility and to sound out their reaction. Without any hesitation, the half-dozen people asked said they would love to become Matthew's godparent, but as we talked further it became clear to me that some would have difficulty making enough time for him. In the end, having picked Rita and Joyce as the final choice, Matthew himself asked them formally to be his god-parents, and of course they agreed.

With all that settled it was a surprise to find Matthew in floods of tears about the christening. 'What's wrong?' I asked. 'I don't want to wear a white dress,' he said. 'What are you talking about Matthew?' 'People have to wear white frilly dresses when they are christened.' Matthew had only ever seen babies christened and I explained that he would be able to wear what he wanted. The tears cleared and Matthew began to look forward to his big day. Father Parkinson heard about the frilly dress episode and roared with laughter. He then told Matthew that he wouldn't be tucking him under his arm to wet his head with the holy water either, because Matthew was a little on the big side.

Matthew's christening (for which he wore a school blazer and flannels) took place on Easter Day in front of a packed congregation. The preparations began at half past seven, when Joyce arrived at the church with a band of helpers loaded down with spring flowers – narcissi, daffodils, a few cream and white and yellow tulips, and hyacinths. On that freezing cold morning, with their fingers numbing by the minute, they transformed the church for this very special Easter Mass.

Fred, Matthew and Lorraine set off just before ten o'clock, while I stayed behind to look after the children, who would have got bored and disrupted the service. They arrived to find the church bathed in yellows, whites and golds from the flowers and altar cloth. I can vouch for the sweet smell of the flowers because one of the arrangements beside the altar was given to Matthew after the service to take back to me. Joyce showed Fred and Lorraine to the front of the church and took Matthew to the sacristy. There she quietly asked if he wanted to go through with the christening. He could back out now, no one would think any the worse of him. Apparently Matthew was calm and assured. He took her hand and said that he wanted very much to be christened.

It was a short ceremony which took place in the middle of Mass. Matthew, Fred, Joyce, Rita and Brian gathered round the font, Matthew and the godparents had said their vows, the holy water was poured gently down Matthew's head and finally Matthew was received into the Church. He was so proud and happy, and the christening was so moving that one of the choir boys let molten wax from the candle he was holding roll down his robe and hand without even noticing what was happening. Matthew was so inspired by the event that he gave Joyce his first spontaneous kiss! I suppose kissing isn't much of a priority in institutions and so Matthew had never been keen on it.

While they were at the service I had been putting the finishing touches to the buffet lunch – ham, salad, jelly, sandwiches, Easter eggs for all the children and, of course, a christening cake for Matthew. It was blue and white and took up most of the centre of our table. The grown-ups got stuck into the food and some wine, but Matthew and all the children pulled off their church clothes and disappeared to the bedroom to play make-believe games of Star Wars.

I asked Matthew what had happened, did he like the service. 'It was OK,' he said gruffly, and I knew that was all I would get out of him for a week or so. If I pushed he would never tell me anything. Sure enough, over the next few days he began to talk about it. However calm he had appeared to Joyce, he had been very nervous; but he was so happy now that he truly belonged, that he was truly part of his Church.

Matthew's faith is powerful, and it gives him an inner strength which helps him face and deal with the trials he has had to suffer. He believes that his faith has also helped him find an extended family: about one week after the christening Matthew said, 'Mum, at one time I had no mum or dad. Now I've got lots.'

CHAMPION CHILD

Matthew has never complained about his looks or his lot. He is determined to lead a completely normal life and so he never asks to have any exceptions made for him, although day-to-day life has been hampered by his webbed trigger fingers which are not as flexible as yours or mine, his cracked dry skin, and his lidless eyes which would bleed and water, making his already poor eyesight worse. We tried contact lenses but they dropped out because Matthew's eyes water so much, and when the optician devised glasses held on by an elasticated band around the back of Matthew's head his skin bled almost constantly.

These problems meant that even apparently straight-forward events, like going to camp with the Cubs, became a major operation. Matthew had joined the Cubs through his school, soon after we had moved to Walmer, and he was intensely proud of his status and uniform. The Scout leaders, Mr and Mrs Goodwin, went out of their way to welcome Matthew into the pack and made sure he was able to join in all their activities. So when the pack went off to camp, which had been set up in a field just outside a small village called Betteshanger, they made sure he would be able to go, too. It was only for a week, and it rained almost constantly every day, but Matthew and the rest of the

Cubs had a ball. The Scout leader let us pick him up once a day, take him home and bathe his skin in the special cream needed to prevent it bleeding too much. We always got him back in time for supper and songs around the camp fire, so he never missed out.

Later that summer, a letter arrived saying that Matthew's latest operation could soon go ahead, but that he would first have to go to London for a check-up and examination. The doctors hoped to be able to build up a pair of ears for Matthew, which would certainly solve many problems. Matthew was very excited even though he had learned through bitter and painful experience to dread surgery. He had already had about a dozen operations; I never knew the exact number because the authorities had never told us and, of course, Matthew was too young to remember some of the early ones. He had had surgery to correct various internal and glandular defects, as well as grafting surgery to give him eyelids. Unfortunately, he had grown out of the eyelids, which is why they no longer closed.

Matthew needed and wanted his physical problems sorted out, but he was scared of everything to do with surgery. He is frightened of injections, too, following painful experiences while he was a toddler, and as far as he is concerned blood tests come into the same category because they involve a needle. We hoped that this spell of surgery would dispel some of his fears and help him forget his bad experiences. We hoped that he would soon be able to treat hospital stays in the same relaxed way that the rest of the family treats them. Unlike many families who regard stays in hospital with horror, a mark of something having gone terribly wrong, they are part of everyday life for us. All the children have odd medical problems which involve going in and out of hospital, so we have learned to turn hospital stays into a sort of holiday for the rest of the family. We pack up our car with games, fizzy drinks, pens and paper, and organize a rota system for visiting the invalid. Fred goes in to see the patient with the first two children, and I stay in the car with the rest of the family and play games and sing songs until it is our turn. We get odd looks from passers-by, but we are used to that now. We told Matthew about our hospital visiting system and reassured him that this time his stay would not be an ordeal.

After a series of tests and examinations in London we were told that the surgery would take place in three stages, slowly rebuilding the ears with skin grafts and cartilage. Matthew went into hospital the following day: at least he knew and liked most of the staff because of his previous surgery at the same hospital. He was less enthusiastic about injections and operations, but determined to go through with it. Cartilage was taken from between his ribs, shaped into ears and then placed under the skin of his skull to settle, soften and heal for a few weeks. Within ten days he returned home, but went back to hospital the following month to have the back of the ears cut into shape, bringing the flap forward to form vestigial ear lobes. The third stage involved grafting skin over the ears and neatening them up. After the second operation, when we went to visit Matthew, I remember seeing this tiny boy, covered in bandages and crying his heart out. I wished I had refused to let the operation go ahead. But I knew this was what he wanted and what the doctors had advised. That was all very reasonable but it didn't remove the guilt.

A few days after he came back from the hospital I began to wish the fortnight would get a move on – by this time Matthew was no longer sore, just very bored and anxious to get back to school and all his friends. He had recovered well from the surgery, and he had no way of using up his excess energy, apart from demanding full-time attention from me during the day while the rest of the family was at school.

Unveiling day finally came. Soon after the children went to school, the district nurse arrived and called Matthew into our tiny kitchen. She washed her hands, laid a sterile cloth across the table, on to which she put two disposable pots filled with cleansing fluid, gauze and tape in sterile wrappings, scissors and tweezers. She sat Matthew in a chair in front of the table and started to unwind the bandages around his head until only two pieces of gauze stood between the new ears and the outside world. She bathed them away, dropping the dressings in a plastic bag. Matthew leapt up and grabbed the mirror I kept on the windowsill above the sink. Words will never be able to describe his look of disappointment and hurt. The ears were a disaster. One was higher than the other so they were impractical as far as glasses went, and they were huge and ungainly. They looked more like cauliflowers than ears. I heard myself saying that they were just a little swollen and that it would be a few days before we would be able to judge how they had turned out. But even the district nurse looked surprised. They were not right, nor would they ever be right if they were left like that. For the first time in his life Matthew cried about his looks. He refused to go out without his anorak hood pulled around his head. His confidence had taken quite a blow.

There was no need to worry about how all Matthew's new friends would react, though; they welcomed him back with pure, child-like innocence. To them he was just their old friend Matthew, odd ears or not. All the same, we rang the headmaster, Mr Seller, to explain what had happened. He told me that he wanted to talk to us anyway and explained that he had decided to enter Matthew in the 'Child Overcoming Adversity' section of the Dr Barnardo's Rumbelows Champion Children Award, because of the way he coped with his disfigurement without a murmur of complaint.

Matthew, along with two other children, won the award. We heard the news just a few weeks after finding out that he had been entered and it could not have come at a better time – just when his confidence needed a boost. On top of that, it gave the three of us a wonderful weekend away from it all. We were invited to London to receive the award, which was to be presented by Princess Margaret. The competition organizers put us up in a splendid hotel in the centre of London not far from Buckingham Palace. It was the first time Matthew had stayed in an hotel and so we arranged for him to sleep in our room. Sure enough, an all-too-familiar pattern began. As soon as the taxi left us in the hotel foyer Matthew, who had been chatting away, became very quiet. His eyes darted everywhere, taking everything and everyone in, watching everyone's every movement. Then, suddenly, he relaxed and the questions started: Why are there two dining-rooms? Why does a man have to operate the lift? Why did you have to give your name to the man behind the desk? Why is the bathroom nearly in the bedroom? Why? Why? Why?

Staying in the same hotel were the rest of the children who were going to receive awards. Some of them were clever or courageous, some of them were brave, some especially talented in music or drama or dance, but they were all modest, a little nervous and very overawed by the prospect of meeting Royalty in front of lots of people. The presentation took place after lunch at the Savoy with Princess Margaret, who gave Matthew – and the rest of the children – a signed parchment.

At the beginning of lunch, a film was shown about each of the children who had won an award, followed by a brief appreciation of how and why each child had been singled out. Then the child, who was usually by this time struck dumb, was given the award by Princess Margaret, who was guided to the winners by her aides. I was astonished at how small she is – she looks so much bigger on television. She congratulated Matthew on his courage and gave him a huge smile, but he was so overcome that he could only just manage to say 'Thank you'. My eyes filled with tears, it was such a proud moment. It was such a special day. There were stars like Bonnie Langford, Keith Harris – who taught Matthew how to blow peas off his knife – and Orville, Christopher Timothy, Teasie Weasie Raymond, Bob Champion, Patricia Hodge, Dr Rob Buckman and Nerys Hughes to name but a few, and all of them went out of their way to make a memorable day for us just by introducing themselves and having long chats with Matthew.

We arrived back to be hailed as celebrities by TVS, our local television station, and all the local newspapers, which carried pictures of Matthew and the rest of us. TVS filmed Matthew at school and at home. It was the first time that all the family had come into contact with the media. Little did we know that this was just the beginning of our relationship with newspapers, television teams and radio stations.

BOY DAVID

A few months after the award ceremony I noticed a startling change in Matthew. He had begun to take increasing interest in and care about his looks. It started when he told me he could only wear one kind of sweatshirt, then he wanted special makes of running shoe, then a new style of trouser. Matthew even learned to brush his few strands of hair across the top of his almost bald head, toupee-style.

Most mothers rejoice when their wild young sons start growing up enough to take some interest in clothes and their appearance. I remember the relief I felt when Kevin and Steve began changing their clothes without being told, and began to resist the temptation to play football or climb trees in their best clothes. But as soon as Matthew started to take more interest in his appearance, I started to worry. Was his concern about his looks going to get in the way of making friends – and girlfriends? Over the years we had managed to steer him away from self-consciousness about his looks and had encouraged him instead to enjoy being himself: a popular, likeable, energetic person. It had worked, but as Matthew approached adolescence his image of himself changed and faltered. He still never complained, but he did start to ask for more details about why he was born looking so different from everyone else, and he wanted to know if anyone would ever be able to help him over some of his problems. We talked to him, we talked to his school and to his doctors, but the general feeling was that little could be done. We were left with a feeling of helplessness, made worse by the ears episode which had knocked Matthew's confidence sideways as well as destroying his faith in the medical profession.

We decided that, for the time being, we would have to concentrate on rebuilding Matthew's confidence. It was as if we were back at square one with Matthew, as if he were back to the stage when he first arrived to stay with us – he was so under-confident then, so unsure about the reaction outsiders would have to his appearance, that if strangers were in sight he would walk and sit with his head bowed to avoid showing his face. We had worked so hard to get him to stop doing that, and now, all over again, we were going to have to counsel Matthew into accepting his appearance and his physical problems before another bout of surgery which was, almost certainly, imminent. Matthew needed further surgery to help him through his normal adolescent development, to give him eyelids, sort out his hands and possibly even sort out his ears. In other words, he needed several operations just to make his day-to-day life easier rather than making any substantial difference to his looks.

Our careful, cautious plans for Matthew were wrecked by a television programme called 'The Boy David'. It was 1984 and Matthew was about ten. One evening, we happened to be watching a Desmond Wilcox documentary about a severely disfigured Peruvian boy named David. David was adopted by a Scottish surgeon, Ian Jackson, who works and lives in the States; taken to the Jacksons' home town in Minnesota and given remarkable and extensive surgery by the surgeon. Matthew and I sat in front of the television that night watching a miracle unfold in front of our eyes, as Professor Jackson rebuilt David's face from a blob of flesh, with a great hole at its centre in place of a mouth, to a fairly normal-looking boy. We sat in silence, soaking in each word and picture, reading each other's thoughts. As the last credit faded on the screen, Matthew turned to me and said, 'He could help me, mum.'

I swallowed hard. 'I don't know about that,' I replied. 'I wanted you to see the film so that you could see another boy who does not look like everybody else.' I had not expected the documentary to show such an astonishing transformation, nor could I see any way of getting the same treatment for Matthew. I felt we were letting him down. But the documentary had a positive effect: watching it seemed to release something in Matthew that made it easier for him to talk to me about his fears and hopes for the future. That night and several subsequent evenings he and I sat up into the small hours talking about his deepest worries: How would he cope when he grew up and moved away from us? Would he be able to get a job? Would friends accept him as he grew older? He was more concerned than we had realized about how he would fit into the grown-up world ahead of him, and, just as I had anticipated, he was worried about how he would get on with girls. There was no concrete help that we could offer, but at least it gave us a chance to talk properly and for him to get a few problems off his chest.

I thought a lot about that film in the coming weeks. Even if it were medically possible to help Matthew with the extensive surgery carried out on Boy David, there was no way we would be able to pay for the treatment. The miners' strike had left Fred redundant. We managed, but with difficulty, from week to week, and the financial problems on top of his redundancy were a strain on all the family. At least the strike in Kent had not been as violent as in the north – our communities were still intact.

For one year the Kent miners remained solid and stayed on strike. I wouldn't let Fred go on picket duty because I was scared about the consequences any injury would have on the family, let alone Fred himself. I have never learned to drive so if he were arrested or injured I wouldn't be able to ferry the children about or do the bulk-buy shopping our family needs. It was selfish, I know, but I felt I had to put the family first. Luckily, Fred's fellow miners were understanding; they knew what our situation was and he was never ostracized like miners elsewhere. In fact, in a way the strike brought our community together. We had to help each other morally and physically in order to survive that year of uncertainty and worry, when no one was sure where the next meal would come from or indeed what would be happening from one day to the next. The policing of the strike was not as extreme in Kent as it was in the north, which helped reduce the bitterness caused by the strike, but all the same it was not an easy time.

While Fred was a miner he brought home £80 a week after stoppages; as soon as the strike began that money naturally stopped. We received £21 family allowance plus £100 total for our foster children; but we were still £80 a week down on our normal income during the strike. The miners' wives support group gave us a total of five food parcels, containing baked beans, fruit or whatever had been donated, and I arranged to pay gas and electricity bills in weekly instalments of about fifty pence rather than try to tackle each one as it came in – so long as you do that and keep up the payments, they do not cut you off. We never went hungry because friends and neighbours gathered round and gave us food and provisions, and Steve and Kevin, our two

boys, sent us money to help cover bills. We wouldn't
have managed otherwise. The neighbours would turn
up without any warning, loaded down with lettuces,
potatoes, tomatoes, raspberries and apples from their
gardens and allotments. Kent is not called the Garden
of England for nothing! And sometimes they would
bring flour and tinned food, too, saying they had a
surplus. Of course they hadn't, but we always
accepted their gifts. They were offerings from true
friends and given in such a way that we were never
made to feel humble. I doubt whether the children
noticed much about the strike because they never went
without. The only difference to them was the fact that
Fred was around the house for most of the time.

I had never wanted Kevin or Steve to follow Fred
down the mines. It is dirty, dangerous work. I wasn't
too keen on Fred doing it either, but there wasn't
much choice. After coming out of the Army, he had
managed to get a job in a chemicals firm, but a couple
of years later he was laid off. They were cutting back
and it was a case of last in, first out. There wasn't
much work about, but Fred had been a miner briefly
when he left school and before going into the Army; so
he had the experience to get a job down the mine.
Kevin had always wanted to go into the Army, ever
since he was a lad. Steve, however, had not been so
sure, but when it came to him finding a job there
weren't many vacancies and finally he decided that
he would be happy in the Army. The strike made me
even more relieved that neither of my natural sons was
a miner.

Towards the end of the strike it became clear that
Fred would be offered redundancy, and in a way that
year had given us a chance to sample what life would
be like if Fred no longer went out to work every day.
We had enjoyed the arrangement despite all the
money worries, and, after a lot of heart-searching and

talking to all the children, we decided to accept redundancy. As soon as Fred had been made redundant we worked out a careful financial strategy to make the best of what little we had. With the redundancy pay we managed to put down a small deposit on our council house, buy three new beds and have a kitchen fitted. I had figured it out very carefully and then been through the figures in detail with Fred. For just a few pounds more than we paid each week in rent we would be able to take on a mortgage. We were both prepared to scrimp and do without for the sake of buying our house, so that the children would have at least some security when we have gone. Redundant or not, we would do it using the fostering assistance allowance. Neither Fred nor I are easily defeated and so we decided once again to fight.

We got a small allowance for the three fostered children and I managed to make a little extra money by selling soft toys and clothes. I daydreamed of money-making schemes constantly, but now more than ever we needed money if Matthew was going to have a chance to be seen by the Boy David surgeon, Ian Jackson. Finally, I decided to put aside four hours every day when the kids had gone to school to make toys to raise money for whatever help we could give Matthew. I doubted we would be able to contact the surgeon in the documentary – I didn't even have his address – but I sent him a letter anyway, addressed to:

Dr I Jackson,
Mayo Clinic,
Minnesota,
USA

It explained everything I knew of Matthew's medical condition, and I enclosed a photograph of Matthew.

Several weeks later came a letter which was to cause me hope, joy, fury and depression. On first reading, it was a wonderful letter from Ian Jackson, the man we had watched at work in the Desmond Wilcox documentary: he said that if we could take Matthew to see him at his surgery in the Mayo Clinic in Minnesota, so that he could feel Matthew's skin and carry out tests, he would tell us whether or not he could help. He made it very clear that he had no way of telling whether or not he could help until they had met. How on earth were we, a redundant miner, an ex-nurse and a higgledy-piggledy family of fostered and adopted kids going to raise the money to get Matthew to Ian Jackson? And even if we did raise the money perhaps we would have our hopes dashed after that first meeting. Perhaps that would do Matthew more harm than good. I tossed and turned for several nights, and talked it through with Fred. We decided not to raise Matthew's hopes at this stage. We would try to take on any extra work we could find to raise money, we would scrimp and save, and when we had the money we would tell Matthew of our plan.

It was not going to be easy. For the first time in my life I began to feel angry about the injustices of the world. I felt cross with ladies in supermarkets who cram their baskets full of the most expensive food and pretend to be helpless, saying 'Oh, but I've never put a plug on a wire' and that sort of thing. I fumed away, getting crosser and crosser with the world: I was irritable with Fred for having a conversation two rooms away, with the family for taking me for granted, with some people I've met for pretending to be what they are not. I festered away to myself, but the root of the problem was simply this: all my son wanted was enough money to have a face which smiled, eyes, ears and a nose which functioned and which supported glasses, and hands which worked properly. It didn't

73

seem much to ask in a world where so many rich people all around me were wasting money on trivia. I felt angry and depressed. I felt like the worst mother in the world. Perhaps I wasn't fit to be Matthew's mum.

FUND-RAISING CIRCUS

In our family no one can wallow in self-pity. There isn't time and, anyway, with kids like ours you can't be sad for long. Matthew was getting on with life as usual and putting a brave face on his inner hurt, so I decided to pull myself together. A morale boost was just around the corner, and the news of it came through Mr and Mrs Goodwin, Matthew's Scout leaders. They rang to say that Matthew had won a marvellous Scouts award, the 'Cornwall Badge' for bravery and endurance. It is rarely given, and it is the country's foremost Scouting accolade. It is the most prestigious award a Scout can win, and in Matthew's case was an acknowledgement of the way he had joined in all his Scouting activities despite his problems – we were very proud of him. We were invited to the presentation ceremony at the Royal Marines barracks in Deal, where Scout leaders from all over the south were to honour Matthew in a special televised ceremony. It was a huge hall with Scouts badges and insignia lining the walls. Fred and I were given VIP seats in the front row.

The presentation was made by Sir Steuart and Lady Pringle. Sir Steuart, who had to have a leg amputated after being the victim of an IRA bomb attack, knows all about having to endure pain, and so he could speak to

Matthew with great understanding. He had a chat with each of the Cubs lined up for inspection before the presentation and then, after making a short speech about Matthew, and the award, he nodded to two Sea Scouts to march forward with Matthew between them. The three boys saluted and Sir Steuart Pringle pinned the gold badge on Matthew's chest. Matthew said thank you but I could see that he was going through one of his phases of wondering what all the fuss was about. He doesn't regard himself as having done anything especially interesting or unusual. Once again, I marvelled at the way Matthew takes his place in the world. Sometimes he is quite shy, particularly with strangers, but he somehow gives courage and confidence to others. He has an inner strength which I sometimes doubt I have.

As usual a lot of the people there, too embarrassed to ask Matthew direct, asked me what had happened to his face and hands. People usually assume he has been terribly burnt. I told them, and when they asked if anything could be done to help him I found myself talking about my dream of sending him to America. Matthew's godparents overheard and we joked about winning the pools. But that passing comment was to change all our lives because, from that moment, news of my idea spread like wildfire through the network of people who had taken Matthew under their wing. From a tiny dream, the idea was turned into a major event. There wasn't one person in particular who decided that Kent should begin a fund-raising campaign for Matthew, it just happened and snowballed. The church, the school, the Scouts, friends, everyone, came up with ideas to raise money.

That weekend Matthew went to stay with Rita, Brian, Darren and Paul, as he often did. As usual, there were other people staying, among them a full-time fireman called Bob Monk. He had met Matthew before, although only briefly, and when the family told him of our dream of sending Matthew to America Bob Monk threw himself behind the fund-raising effort. It was quite something to see Bob swing into action. He is six feet tall and muscle-bound, with enough determination and energy to make the craziest scheme work. In his years as a fireman he and his colleagues had done plenty of fund-raising, so he was to lift our efforts out of the small group of friends and contacts into a wider circuit. The night he came to see us for the first time, just a few days later, he said as he left that he and the lads would help. That was an understatement. Our world was about to be turned upside down. He was talking in terms of thousand of pounds and somehow it seemed unreal. He seemed in such a rush about everything, too, that although I liked and trusted him I didn't really think he would be able to do the things he was talking about. I liked the way he seemed so determined to help, but I remained cautious – I'm a typical Virgoan I suppose, feet on the ground.

Leaving us to make soft toys and arrange jumble sales, Bob activated his well-tried fund-raising circuit by trudging around local shops, asking for raffle prizes and donations, bullying his own friends and neighbours into helping, and writing letters to large and small firms in the area. One of Bob's contacts was Phil Oliver, who owned the Kingsdown Country Club in Deal. When Phil heard what we were trying to do, he said that if we could organize some events he would let us use his premises for five consecutive days without charge. I was astonished by his generosity. The club was based in a fine old manor house set in its own grounds. On the second floor there was a large restaurant and on the floor below a dance floor, a stage, a bar decorated with seafaring themes – ships' bells, nets, ships' wheels, and pictures of boats, ships and seascapes. It was a lovely place, but how on earth would I fill the country club, which could take hundreds of people, for five days running? Bob took it in his stride and said he would have no problems. Meanwhile his wife Irene became a fund-raiser's widow, while their daughter Laura only had a part-time dad.

Now, as I've explained, life in the Learoyd household has never been straightforward or simple. But from the day the fund-raising really got under way, every single waking moment was mayhem. Bob, Irene and Laura were frequent visitors and both our houses became sorting offices for ideas, donations, gifts of prizes, and letters asking for help from companies and individuals. Everyone gave their services free and everything, down to the entrance fees collected each day, was put in Matthew's fund.

The fund-raising happened in a headlong rush. Bob Monk had got in touch with us in December; the very first event, the boot fair, was on 23 February, 1986; and that evening we launched the country club week with a dance session and a Wild West show. Needless to say, the weather did its worst. It didn't actually snow but there was the kind of bone-chilling wind that only those on the east coast know about. Four brave Brownies faced that wind all day, having vowed not to leave their posts until they had made £100 by selling the jumble they had been collecting since Christmas. The youngest was eight, the oldest ten, and their generous determination made me feel grateful and very, very humble. That night the club held a Wild West show – sharpshooters, cowboys hats and boots, and plenty of 'Yeehaaing!' which kept Matthew happy. Better still, he was presented with a gun mounted on a wooden plaque and he was made an honorary member of the local Wild West club which had organized the event.

The second night was given over to a ladies' fashion

show and a hairdressing display. On 25 February there was a pub games night, and a disco night with Invicta Radio; on the following night the Boogi Band ran a dance night; and on the final night we had a Royal Marines Band concert and a firemen's majorette dance display. Yes, really, those big, burly firemen donned incredibly large frilly white knickers (I had to make them because it was impossible to buy ones large enough), firemen's boots, tutus and white fur hats. They twirled broomsticks and cancanned to an audience of about a thousand people, including the Mayor and Mayoress of Deal and all the top brass of the Kent fire brigade. Local firms had given some splendid prizes like a holiday in Barbados, a microwave oven, and a boat trip, which meant that the first major week of Matthew's fund-raising events was almost bound to be a success. It was. We raised £6,000.

Everyone put in time, effort and goodwill, and many of the fund-raisers and helpers thought of really creative ways in which to help. Acorn Computers, for instance, gave Matthew a BBC micro-computer complete with a colour monitor, tapes and disc drives, to help with his education. That was the idea, at least, and it has certainly helped Matthew become computer literate, although I'm not sure how much school work he does on it. The computer tends to be used as a games machine. Firms and individuals had been so kind that, whenever possible, we let Matthew stay up late or be driven quite long distances so that he and Fred could thank the fund-raisers and well-wishers in person for their time and effort.

A kindly whirlwind had swept us along for several weeks, but I was aware that the rest of the family was becoming increasingly jealous. They saw all the extra fuss being made of Matthew, they saw the presents and honours he was getting and they knew that he might have something done to help his problems. So why couldn't they have something to help them over their problems? And why couldn't they have some presents too? Why couldn't they stay up beyond bedtime like Matthew to go to some of the events? It wasn't easy and, without ever saying that there was little any of us could do to help them around their physical and mental problems beyond what we were already doing, we just made a greater effort to give the rest of the family extra treats at weekends. And whenever possible we involved them in some of the fun of the fund-raising. Sometimes the Press or members of the public took pictures of all the children, and sent those pictures to us. That would cheer up the kids no end, because they could never understand why everyone always wanted pictures of Matthew and never of them.

As a result of the publicity generated by the five-day event, the fund-raising effort gathered momentum. Luckily we didn't often have to worry about keeping Matthew's feet on the ground. He rarely got big-headed, despite all the attention and all the presents he was getting. He would come home from whatever event he had been to, tell us a little about it and then forget it, completely – just put it to one side and get on with life as brother to lots of boys and girls. The few times his new-found fame went to his head were when he was tired. One Saturday afternoon, after a week during which Matthew had stayed up late to go to several fund-raising events, I found him in his bedroom doing the kind of thing he used to do when he first arrived with us. He was terrorizing poor Ben and Simon by pulling faces at them, lurching forward to stare right into their faces, and saying things like, 'They gave me a special badge last night but they didn't give you anything. And they aren't giving any money to you to go to America.' He was even gloating about the number of cups of Ribena and Coke he'd

A stable home environment was something Matthew had always longed for; his dream was realized when he became a special member of a very special family. He is seen here with his mum and dad, Christine and Fred Learoyd, his brother Ben and sisters Lucy (left) and Sarah.
David Graves/The People

Matthew has always been popular at school. Here his classmates at the Roman Catholic school in Walmer give him a rousing cheer.
David Graves/The People

Champion child: Matthew receives his Dr Barnardo's Rumbelows Champion Children Award and gets the chance to meet TV celebrities such as Christopher Timothy (left), Matthew Kelly and Nerys Hughes.

The Harrington pub in Derby was just one of the many groups up and down the country that raised money for Matthew's trust fund.
Raymonds Photographers, Derby

Matthew soon earned himself the nickname 'one-take' for his ability to give off-the-cuff interviews. Constant media attention was something he learned to take in his stride.   *Mike Griggs/Dover Express*

A moment of anguish and anticipation: Matthew and Fred say goodbye to the rest of the family as they set off for America and their first meeting with the Boy David surgeon, Ian Jackson.   *Mike Griggs/Dover Express*

The cool jet-setter: Matthew enjoys VIP status on his first flight to America and is allowed a privileged visit to the cockpit to meet the captain and crew. *David Graves/The People*

Matthew and Fred were made welcome wherever they went in America, but Earl McGee (left) and his wife Anna became special friends. *David Graves/The People*

A trip to Disney World and more dreams come true for Matthew. Meeting a full-size Mickey Mouse was bettered only by his favourite 'ride' – miniature racing cars on a circuit – which he went on at least ten times!
David Graves/The People

Firemen from both sides of the Atlantic: The Kent fire-fighters (above),
headed by Bob Monk (second from right), worked hard to raise funds for
Matthew and enlisted the help of their counterparts in Rochester, USA, to
make Matthew's visit so memorable.
Mike Griggs/Dover Express   David Graves/The People

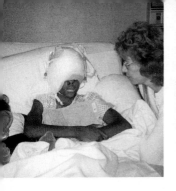

After his second round of operations at the Mayo Clinic, Matthew is comforted by Christine along with his favourite toy – the cuddly monkey Fred bought him on their first trip. And it didn't take Matthew long to regain his appetite!   *Christine Learoyd*

Top on the list of Matthew's favourite discoveries in the New World was American ice-cream. Here he tucks into one of his famous concoctions.   *David Graves/The People*

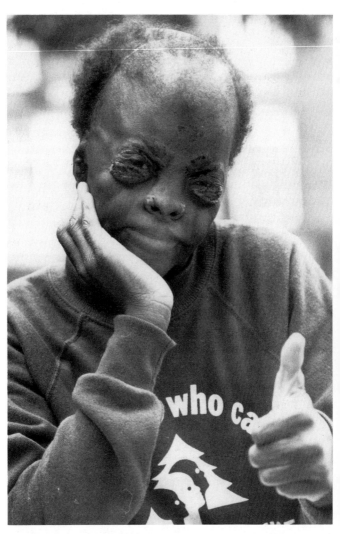

With a string of operations behind him, and the prospect of many more to come, Matthew's spirit and determination still shine through.
Dover Express

been given while they had been stuck at home with me. I was horrified, really surprised at Matthew. His nastiness earned him a rare spanking which seemed to prevent a repeat performance.

It was hard for him, though, because he had suddenly achieved star status in the eyes of the world and yet at home he was still expected to be a son and brother with no special treats or treatment. Sometimes it seemed as if everyone in the world was doing something special for Matthew. Everyone – young, old, rich and poor – was losing weight or doing handstands, or lifting weights or sweating away pounds to raise money for Matthew. At the Thompson Bell pub in Deal the men were sponsored to shave off half their beards for a month. Imagine what they looked like! And Jacky, the landlady, was sponsored to keep silent for one day – no mean feat because she was running the pub. Children gave up their pocket money for him, anonymous donations arrived at his church, St John's, which was also launching a fund-raising effort. Women knitted blankets and made toys to sell for him; pubs, clubs, Brownies, Scouts, Guides and Cubs did everything in their power to help: hiked, put collecting jars on bars, jogged, ran in appalling weather, and someone even provided a kissagram service, all to raise more money for Matthew.

Lorraine, generous to the last, agreed to move back to our house so that she could cook meals for us while I dealt with callers. Lesley, who lived just down the road with her husband Tom and toddler son Michael, had become a great friend and a regular visitor. Now she was to become unofficial gofer, answering calls and helping with letters. Even our hairdresser, Carol, who always came to us instead of making us go to her salon, learned to man the phone while I was under the drier or while she was trying to cut the children's hair.

A pub in Derby, The Harrington, chained their

regulars together in couples and dropped them off a few miles from the pub with instructions to get as far away from the pub as they could without any food or money. Each couple was sponsored and one got as far as France! Even visiting celebrities, like Norman Wisdom, who was doing a spell at our local theatre, could not escape, and they were roped in to make presentations to Matthew by local fund-raising groups. Quite often we never even knew about a local factory or pub or office raising money for Matthew until one of them rang us to say that they had arranged a cheque presentation ceremony. Word had spread like wildfire.

Customs officers at Dover Docks put out buckets decorated with home-made campaign posters for Matthew asking for any loose foreign change from returning tourists, and the local bank agreed to sort it out free of charge. Marks and Spencer and many of the larger firms in the area ran their own events; Matthew's school held raffles, bring-and-buy sales and collections, and many other schools in the area helped. Every shop and business in the area seemed to have a picture of Matthew and a collection box beside it; Bill Bennett, our local butcher, and twenty or so of his running companions, 'The Channel Runners', entered the London Marathon to raise money for him. Later Bill put up a display of Matthew's pictures and posters – the latter were made, free of charge, by Tony Wood and Jimmy Davies just because their children went to the same school as Matthew – and a 'Matthew's campaign totalizer' which crept up the scale day by day. We had worked out that we needed to raise a minimum of £30,000 for the flights and motel bills. But in reality we had no idea – no idea for instance about how expensive American surgery is, especially when it is carried out by one of the world's foremost experts.

Our dream was coming true, but it was happening

so quickly and such large sums of money were involved that we needed to organize things more formally. This is where one of Matthew's Sea Scout leaders offered to create a trust fund. The Scout leader had got to know Matthew when Matthew, aged eleven, moved from being a Cub to a Scout. We lived on the coast and so Matthew automatically became a member of the Sea Scouts, the sea-orientated branch of the Scouting movement. Matthew's Scout leader and his wife, who is also involved with the Scouting movement, had some especially useful skills to offer in that, before retirement, they had been involved in hospital administration. They had also done a great deal of fund-raising for the Scouts, so they were well aware of the pitfalls involved. The Scouting movement was the ideal body to set up Matthew's trust fund and they did so by drawing up a detailed legal document and inviting one or two leading members of the community to be trustees.

We still didn't know whether or not Professor Ian Jackson would be able to help Matthew, but the fund-raising had taken off in such a big way that Matthew's problems, hopes and future had become public property. I couldn't open a newspaper without seeing his face, I couldn't go out shopping without being stopped in the street and asked about Matthew. The fund-raising effort depended on as many people as possible knowing about Matthew's problems and so, in a way, he had become famous, and one of the problems of that fame was the increasing resentment from the other kids. As usual, it was Bob Monk who recognized the problem and decided to do something about it. Early that summer he rang to ask if the family would like to come down to his fire station in Deal for a children's tea party the men were arranging the following week. He said it would give us a chance to meet some of the fire-fighters we had only ever heard about on the fund-raising grapevine, and it would give the kids a chance to make some new friends over Coke and cakes. Bob is a stickler for detail, and he left us precise instructions about when and where to arrive.

I decided not to tell the children until the night before. If I'd told them any further in advance they would have expected the tea party to happen almost immediately, and when it didn't temper tantrums and crying fits would have ensued just because they had got overexcited and then disappointed. They are quite good at understanding twenty-four hours either side of the present, but beyond that they cannot go.

The party was scheduled for early Saturday afternoon. I didn't dress the kids when they woke but let them wander about the house in their pyjamas for the morning so that I wouldn't have to change them again before party time. They loved the idea because they hate dressing. Two hours before we were due to leave the house I started to wash the older kids and sort out their party clothes – their Sunday best. Matthew can look after himself but Eddie needs help. He always tries so hard, and he always manages to wash, but he has so little movement in his legs, and his arms have so little control, that dressing isn't easy. This means that Fred or I have to help him over the last stages of pulling trousers on or off and of getting arms in sleeves.

We have a routine for mass outings. We start with the child able to keep him or herself the cleanest. If Fred does the washing and dressing upstairs I supervise the rest of the family downstairs, and vice versa. As soon as the last, most messy kid is dressed and ready it's our turn to dress, one by one, so that there is always someone looking after the family. We went through the usual routine, finishing with last orders for the loo, and trooped off to the car. Our beige Nova, the replacement for our Hunter which had finally gone to the scrapyard in the sky, was a forgiving machine: we overloaded it on almost every outing and yet it usually kept going. The packing always began with Eddie's wheelchair which went in the boot, followed by Lucy's pushchair, spare nappies, spare towel and trousers just in case. We had got the back seating arrangements down to an art form: Sarah in first with Simon on her lap, followed by Matthew with Ben on his lap, followed by me with Lucy on my lap. The advantage of this arrangement was that no one could fight because no one could move. Fred drove and Eddie rode in the front seat, the doors were squashed shut, and off we would go. This is a feat yet to be recognized by the *Guinness Book of Records*, but I feel sure we deserve a place somewhere there.

Fortunately, the fire station was only about a fifteen-minute drive away. We had been told to park in the yard at the back, and as we swung round the side of the station there were shouts of delight from the kids – the fire engines had been parked out in the yard. It was a bright day and so they looked particularly glamorous, glittering in the sunlight. Simon and Ben's excitement levels had shot straight off the end of the Richter scale. 'Jelly, jelly, jelly I want jelly,' shouted Simon, whose pleasures are simple and straight-forward. Ben was shouting ever more insistently that he wanted to slide down the firemen's pole. As the car drew to a halt Bob Monk appeared, opened the car door and helped us unload, while I gave the family a quick lecture on being good and behaving well. It fell on deaf ears.

But I suddenly realized that beyond the Learoyd bedlam something was not quite right. I looked out of the rear window to see a large crowd, including a TVS team filming our every move. What the heck was going on? I turned towards the crowd to be told by one of the camera crew, 'Just carry on as normal'. We walked towards the fire station doors, which are normally closed; but as we reached them there was a great rattle and groan and they opened to reveal a sea of faces, familiar and strange, and a splendid buffet tea set out on trestle tables down each side of the concrete building. No wonder the fire engines were parked outside.

Even the children were overawed, and for once they were quiet as we were ushered through the crowd to the front of the building where various local dignitaries, including the Mayor and Mayoress of Deal, had gathered. We were being filmed all the time. I still had no idea what was going on, and reached for Fred's hand. He squeezed mine and smiled. At the far end of the fire station we turned to face all the people while Bob Monk made a speech. He said that although everyone knew about Matthew's problems, few knew about the rest of the children. He talked about each of our kids and their special needs, and then said that he and his fellow fire-fighters had decided that it was time someone did something for all the family. A stranger who had been standing beside Bob stepped forward to be introduced to us – it was the managing director of Toyota, who started talking about a van to make travelling easier for us. Everything went rather blank for a moment, although I remember picking Lucy out of her pushchair and sitting in it myself.

Minutes later the crowd was asked to stand back against the walls, and a large white van drove into the fire station. It was to be ours, our very own. The managing director gave the keys to Fred. The crowd started to clap, flashlights were popping and TVS were still filming our every move. It was all I could do not to cry – what a godsend, what a marvellous gift. It would enable us to give all the family more treats. It would give us more of a chance to go out together, it would give us a kind of freedom we had never tasted. It would also help smooth over some of the jealousy which sometimes bubbled up from Matthew's brothers and sisters – now they knew that people cared as much about them as they did about Matthew. Today was their day and they were as much the centre of attention as Matthew.

Fred and I wandered around the crowd thanking everybody, while our kids tucked into the buffet. And there lay the rub. Joyce Deadman, Matthew's godmother, arrived at my elbow to whisper that there was a problem with the van. My heart sank – were they taking it away from us already? No, Simon had been sick over the back seat. It hadn't taken long for the family to bring me down to earth. We cleared up the mess and loaded up the van to go home, leaving the car to be collected the following day. I felt like the Queen sitting there in what seemed to us like a huge automobile, with all the crowds watching and waving as we pulled away. It was a welcome change to be able to see out of the window, to be able to breathe properly thanks to the fact that no one had to sit on anyone's lap. This was luxury. But even our departure was disrupted. Matthew's friend Paul Burrows got his head stuck through the stair rails. At least he had chosen the right place to do it!

I woke early the next morning and, well, I just couldn't resist it. I rushed to the window to look outside and, yes, it was still there. It hadn't been a dream, a Japanese fairy godmother had given us a big white van.

ROYAL PRESENTS

Early in 1986 we were sent a donation from a very unexpected source. We had become used to getting unusual donations, like the touching ones of a few pence from little children who scrawled MATTHEW in big, baby writing across the envelope. But this donation was very special because it came, with a letter, from the Queen Mother. Well, it was written by a member of her household, but it carried the Queen Mother's coat of arms, and it said that Her Majesty wanted to make a donation to his fund. We showed the letter to Matthew who was very pleased, but I don't think he realized how special it was.

It was so kind and unexpected that it was a matter of several weeks before we realized how it might have happened. Soon after Bill Bennett, the butcher, had put up the display about Matthew, a large chauffeur-driven limousine drew up outside his shop, and the driver got out to ask for more details about Matthew's trust fund. This must have been the Queen Mother's driver. Then we realized there was another connection: Matthew had been introduced to the Queen Mother when he was about three and still in hospital; but would she have remembered that little boy from all those years ago? We'll never know. And it was her interest that mattered, however it had come about.

Soon after the Royal donation had arrived a local

agency journalist rang to ask if we would like to have help from a national newspaper. He said he had contacts on Fleet Street and if we agreed he would ring round to see who was interested. I was becoming used to saying yes to everything and so agreed without thinking too hard about it. After all, it was unlikely anyone would be interested, and if they were I could think about it when they got in touch. A few days later Jane Owen, the medical editor of the *People*, rang to ask if she could come to see us with their chief photographer, David Graves. I felt very nervous. I was on my guard both for us and for Matthew himself. I imagined headlines about Matthew being a freak and about us being 'saints' for having taken him in along with all the other children. But Matthew is not a freak and we are not saints. Far from it. We argue and, sometimes, get cross and fed up with the pressure of living with our children, as any parents do. We are just ordinary. Matthew was very excited about being in the paper. And then, as he got used to the idea, he just accepted it as the norm. That seems to be how he copes with life.

Jane seemed nice and understanding; but she had a job to do, a story to write. She asked us so many questions and slowly Matthew's story unfolded. She said that the newspaper would tell the readers where to send donations and that, with a bit of luck, it should raise money for the fund. We needed every penny we could get. Deep down, however, I still had doubts. I decided that we would need the *People*'s help to turn Matthew's dream into a reality, but I didn't want him made out to be some kind of circus exhibit. He was just a boy who had the misfortune to be born with a disfigured face and body. He laughed, cried and felt hurt just like the rest of us. Jane reassured us that she would write about Matthew the boy, not some fictitious freak, for that weekend's paper.

I told all our friends about the *People*'s story and they, like us, waited on tenterhooks for Sunday. I didn't sleep much that Saturday night and, instead, stayed up polishing all our brasswork and worrying about whether or not I had done the right thing. Matthew on the other hand wasn't in the least bit bothered. He was just excited about telling all his friends that he was about to appear in a national newspaper. But it was too late to change my mind now. I'm sure the newspaper boy was late that Sunday but finally there came the telltale thud of the paper arriving. I was first to the doormat, closely followed by all the kids. There, staring back at us, was a picture of Matthew, me and Fred. Matthew's story took up the whole of page eleven. I read quickly and was very moved by the article; it was true to life, not sloppy or self-pitying. It was just our Matthew.

From then on our phone never stopped ringing: long-lost friends who wanted to get back in touch and help; some of Fred's old army pals offering help, and Ben's godmother contacted us after years of silence simply because she had seen our picture in the paper; strangers who wanted to help, fellow fund-raisers with yet more ideas for raising money. Many people were so impressed by what they had read that they wanted to lend a hand or give some money. But that was nothing. By mid-week the post office had been thrown into turmoil by the amount of post we were getting. There were so many letters that they had to organize special deliveries to the National Westminster Bank in Walmer, which had agreed to look after Matthew's trust fund. Letters came from all over England and some from abroad. One was from a man in Africa who had seen a copy of the *People*. But the most exciting development was that, by the end of that first week, *People* readers had sent us £15,833.90. With the money already raised locally we were well on the way to the £30,000 that the trustees had estimated we would need to go to the States.

While we worried over pounds, shillings and pence, Matthew was blissfully unaware of the practicalities of what we were planning. As far as he was concerned he was going to go on an aeroplane to America and get his face fixed, and nothing else mattered. We reminded him constantly that there was a chance that Professor Jackson would not be able to help him, but that was a message Matthew was reluctant to take in.

Trustees from the Scouting movement turned their houses into a sort of office on our behalf. Diligently, they sorted through every single one of the thousands of donations and letters sent to the bank, noting down the name and address of the sender, the amount of the donation, and then sending an individual 'thank you' letter to each and every one – except for the few that came in anonymously, of course. Quite often, especially at the beginning, they had to work through the night to keep up with the post. It was kind and much-needed help. We could not have done it: Learoyd life was only just keeping up with itself. The trustees showed me all the mail every day or so. There were some extraordinary letters, many of which were very moving – they came from prisoners, old people, disabled people and even from some people who had lost children and felt that a donation was more use than flowers. I've now filed some of these letters away at home so that when Matthew is older he will realize how much love surrounds him and how many people care for him.

A second article appeared in the *People* the following weekend to tell the readers how the trust fund was going. This time I felt I could talk to Jane with confidence, and I was not as nervous as I had been the first time round. I knew I could trust her; she was as interested as everyone else to see Matthew's dream come true. The fund-raising was going so well that we started to make concrete arrangements for Matthew to go away. But alongside the astonishing success of the fund-raising came some unexpected problems, one of which was local gossip kindled by jealousy or boredom or heaven knows what. In any small community there is always gossip. The good side of small-town gossip is that if someone has a problem they are not alone. Other people, neighbours mostly, get to know about the problem and they will step in to help if they can. The bad side of gossip is that petty jealousies and rivalries can erupt as soon as someone starts doing particularly well, or if anyone starts doing something unusual. The progress with the fund-raising was getting so much publicity that we were the centre of attention in our own community and in much of the county, and, sure enough, the tittle-tattle began.

A few months after the *People* had run our story, I bought a new sofa. Our old one, which had been second-hand to begin with, had finally given up the ghost. The cushions sagged through to the webbing which had broken, and the springs had started to push their way through to the surface. So I bought a brand new grey velour sofa. The rumour that I had bought it with some of Matthew's fund money began to circulate. I was so angry when I discovered what was being said that I can't even remember who told me about this particular piece of gossip. The rumour was sheer fabrication. In fact, I bought the sofa through a catalogue club which delivers the goods and then collects payments week by week – £5 in this case. It was the only way of getting the new sofa. At the time our own income was so low I couldn't afford new clothes.

It doesn't sound any big deal, does it? But the problem was that, although all our friends know we are meticulously honest about funds of any kind, I felt hurt that anyone should question our honesty, and I felt worried that fund-raisers who did not know us personally would believe what was being said. I needn't have worried. The rumours were put about by one or two miseries, but the majority ignored the rumours and carried right on fund-raising for all they were worth. In shops, storekeepers would recognize us from television or newspaper stories and come up to Matthew to wish him luck. I wished I could ignore the rumours as easily as they could and, although Fred constantly told me not to listen to the silly things that were being whispered, they still upset me.

The rumours came to a head a few months later. Fred has always liked his beer and darts. It's his one little luxury, his one means of escaping from this madhouse. So his routine for spending a night with the lads every now and then hadn't changed during the fund-raising period but, inevitably I suppose, one or two trouble-makers started to suggest that he was drinking away Matthew's fund. It would have been impossible for Fred to do that. All the money for the trust fund went straight into the bank after the doner's name and address had been noted down by the Scout volunteers. Sometimes individuals would turn up on our doorstep instead of sending the money to the bank and leave a cheque or an envelope with cash, but we would simply wait for our daily visit from one of the trustees and hand it over to them intact. But the same rumour-mongers suggested that we weren't handing over all the money. What could we do? Apart from inviting witnesses to live with us in our already cramped house, and to watch every transaction, there was nothing we could do except to continue to be as careful with money as we always were.

I discovered the main source of the rumours but I wanted to avoid direct confrontation. I didn't think it would help because, as I've already explained, there was no obvious way of disproving what was being said. We just had to rely on the fact that most people knew us well enough to know that the rumours were rubbish. But in the end I could stand it no longer, and I rang one of the main culprits. It was not a satisfactory conversation. I got cross and asked for an end to the gossip. The culprit was patronizing and cruel, suggesting that I was just an ill-read ignoramus who didn't know what she was talking about. It was stalemate unless we went to the courts, and I had enough on my plate without getting involved in that kind of game. Added to which, we wouldn't have had the money to go to court – unless of course we'd used up some of the fund!

There was another, more understandable, rumour about us: it was actually more opinion than rumour. Many people felt that Matthew should not be allowed to go to all the fund-raising events. It was widely known through feature articles on him, and through his classmates, that Matthew was very behind with his school work. Some people felt that he ought to be giving his undivided attention to that rather than spending some evenings at events, some of which went on quite late. Well, I don't suppose he gave his best in class after one of those evenings but Matthew is an unusual boy and, even by his standards, the events happening around him were unique, unusual and entirely central to him. They were as much a part of his future as his school work but, unlike academic work to which he could return at any time during his life, these were one-off events. They were things created specially for him, and Fred thought it important that Matthew should see the events, and that the people who had gone to so much trouble to raise money for him should be given a chance to meet him.

Hurtful remarks still filtered back to us, like: the Learoyds are exploiting Matthew for the sake of publicity. That was nonsense, but I sometimes worried about his school work, and tried to talk to Fred about it. But Fred was so angry about the rumours that he had dug his heels in and he refused at first to discuss my worries. I think he believed that I was just reacting to the gossip. I wasn't; I, too, was worried about the number of events we should let Matthew attend. One Wednesday, two days after Matthew had stayed up until half past ten at Dover Girls Grammar, where a group called The Rock Gospel played for Matthew and raised several thousand pounds, Fred wanted Matthew to go out again, this time to a cheque presentation at a local pub. 'He's too tired,' I said. 'He's not, he's only young and he can take it,' replied Fred. 'But I want to go. I *promised* I'd go,' chipped in Matthew. 'Go to your room please, Matthew, while your dad and I talk.'

'He's going, we promised and that's all there is to it. Just because you are always busy in the evenings it doesn't mean to say we can't go out and enjoy ourselves. You're getting to be a bloody miserable woman,' said Fred, whose voice had gone up a pitch or two. 'You want to spend more time out than here now that you've found fame and all your fine new friends,' I retorted. 'Shut up, get ready and come with us instead of moaning,' came Fred's answer. 'I don't want to go.' This was getting stupid, but we'd taken our sides in the ring and nothing would stop us now. 'No, you never want to come out so stop going on about it. You take too much notice of what other people say,' said Fred as he stormed out of the room and yelled upstairs to Matthew, telling him to be ready within ten minutes.

Ben, woken by our row, appeared in his pyjamas and I snapped at him to get straight back to bed. Ten minutes later the front door banged and Fred and Matthew were gone, leaving me alone, deflated and in tears. Of course it wasn't really Fred's fault. But which of us was right? Was I letting the gossip get to me, as Fred had said, or did I have a point when I said that Matthew was going to too many events? I wondered how they were getting on and at least felt grateful that all the people at the pub would see how grateful Matthew and Fred were. I felt guilty about snapping at Ben and popped upstairs to tuck him in and say sorry. Ben had become obsessed with fund-raising, and I remember one day discovering him knocking on a neighbour's door with a pen and pad asking for money for his own trust fund. In fact, he tried this once or twice so, again, we had to try to explain to him that although Matthew had a trust fund it did not mean he had more love than Ben. It wasn't easy for any of the children to understand.

Lorraine had to put up with a lot of tension and bickering caused by the fund-raising because she spent almost every day at our house helping out, looking after the children and running the household while I dealt with phone calls and the fund-raisers. There were several moments when I found myself shouting at her with no cause. 'You haven't wiped the children's faces properly.' 'Why haven't you kept the fire stoked up?' 'Haven't you done the washing-up yet?' We would end up having a blazing row followed by her rapid exit:

'That's it, I'm going home. I've only got one pair of hands and I don't *have* to help you . . .'

That was the worst part of the tension and tiredness – I took it out on those I loved most. Looking back on that period, I think I was offhand, even rude, to some of our closest friends, although none of them ever said anything, and today they are still close enough to have stayed friends. Which shows what good friends they are! Life was exciting but it was tense, and although I usually managed to hold my peace when public gossip started there were moments when I just wanted to scream: 'OK, I'm smiling at you now and nodding in an understanding way and in a moment I'll explain the truth behind the rumours – but stop hurting me. I'm just human and ordinary, just like you, and I'm simply trying to do my best for my family.'

While we had been busy with the trust fund and all its attendant pleasures and problems, Matthew's social worker from Parents for Children, Hadi Argent, had won a Churchill scholarship to go to Minnesota in the USA, the very place that Professor Ian Jackson, Matthew's surgeon, worked. I don't know whether or not it was coincidence, but it was a boon to us. Hadi arranged to meet the surgeon and his family and explain Matthew's problems to them face to face. At about the same time a lady called Christine Piff, who founded a self-help group called 'Let's Face It' for facially disfigured people, wrote to Ian Jackson to explain Matthew's problems. 'Let's Face It' helps people come to terms with facial disfigurements, and we had been put in touch by Matthew's adoption agency when he first came to live with us. Neither Christine nor Hadi got much further than I had because, as Ian Jackson pointed out, he could not guarantee any help until he had examined Matthew, but it helped to have further letters from him expressing an interest and saying he would help as much as he could.

Preparations for Matthew's trip to the States began in earnest in early May, just five months after we had begun fund-raising. We made a series of phone calls to the clinic in Minnesota, although it was a while before we got used to phoning at night – their morning – to overcome the time difference. One of us was going to have to accompany Matthew, and Fred was the obvious choice. He had travelled the world with the Army and could find his way around anywhere.

Added to which I don't like to think what would have happened if I had left Fred in charge at home. He is very good at looking after the children for a day or so but he never gets round to some jobs, so I would certainly have returned to mounds of ironing, quite a lot of washing, dusty shelves and dirty floors!

We had discussed our plans for Matthew fairly openly from the beginning and all the rest of the children knew what was happening. There was no sudden announcement about him going away, and no shock for any of the children about Fred going with him. We set the departure date for 20 May and then realized that Matthew, who had only ever been to France, had an annual passport which was about to expire, with only two weeks to go before departure day. He certainly didn't have a visa. Neither did Fred, so they had to go to London in person rather than making an application by post. Fred had to go twice in the end. He thought he would be able to get the passports there and then, but he arrived at the embassy to find that he had to leave the passports and collect them a week later. Even then the queuing took up the whole day, but at least he and Matthew had their visas. They also needed new light clothes because by May Minnesota would probably have temperatures in the 100s. Fred and Matthew loathe shopping but they gritted their teeth, trooped off to Deal and managed to get everything they needed in the space of three hours.

Bob Monk meanwhile had become increasingly involved in arrangements on both sides of the Atlantic. He continued to coordinate fund-raising in the UK while in America he alerted fellow fire-fighters to look after Matthew, to raise money for him and to be on hand if he needed help of any kind out there. Scout leaders in Kent alerted the Scout movement in America, so gradually everyone was getting ready to welcome Matthew and Fred. At school the children clubbed together to buy Matthew a tape recorder and some tapes so that he could keep them in touch with his progress even when he wasn't up to writing letters – and they would be able to send him taped messages, too.

As the leaving date drew nearer, Matthew became increasingly nervous or excited, switching from one emotion to the other, day to day. We reminded him that he shouldn't let his hopes rise too far, and we told him that even if that doctor couldn't help we would carry on trying to find someone who would be able to. But above all we told him over and over again how much we loved him. We told him that there would always be plenty of cuddles and lots of love for him, new face or not. We promised that one way or another his medical problems would be sorted out.

I packed and repacked two navy blue cases on wheels for Matthew and Fred. Fred's luggage was pretty straightforward. Matthew's had to include crucial things like a battered teddy called Checky, which had a faded checkered body, light-brown paws and a head stained with blood despite many careful washing sessions. Checky really belonged to Ben but, every time Matthew went into hospital for surgery, Ben lent him Checky, hence the blood stains. It was a great honour for Matthew to be able to take Checky so far away from Ben. The other crucial part of the luggage, as far as Matthew was concerned, was his Lego set, pens, drawing pads, rubber and felt tips, which still give him enormous pleasure. I think that if I'd failed to pack any one of those special toys, Matthew would probably have got on the next plane back home.

Fred stowed passports, visas, travellers cheques and credit cards in his pockets, leaving a few travellers cheques in his luggage, just in case his pockets sprang a leak. At about ten o'clock in the morning on 20 May I said goodbye to them both. It was quite a send-off party: a dozen or so neighbours, the family and a camera crew from TVS. I could hardly bear to wave as Bob Monk drove them away: what would happen to my little boy? Lorraine was going to stay with me full-time for the coming weeks while Fred and Matthew were away. I didn't even know how long they would be gone. If they were away a long time I would miss them a great deal, but if they were away only a few days my heart would be broken because it would mean the surgeon couldn't help Matthew.

Matthew was met at Gatwick Airport by Jane Owen and David Graves from the *People*, who were going to spend the first few days with Matthew and Fred. Just before they boarded, Philip Hornby from TVS asked Matthew what he would miss most while he was away. Matthew shrugged and said 'My Mum'. I watched the interview that evening on the local TVS news show, 'Coast to Coast', with the tears rolling down my face. He looked so small and vulnerable.

LIFT-OFF

For seven weeks I knew what was happening to
Matthew only second-hand: Fred rang me once a day
without fail, even if that meant the call coming
through at two in the morning my time; Matthew rang
when he wasn't in surgery or going for tests, and the
local newspapers and television, the *People* and the
local radio station, Invicta, kept regular checks on his
progress. It was odd to think that strangers often knew
before I did what was happening to my son. I didn't
like having to hear so much news second-hand, and I
would have preferred to be there myself. Fred helped
by keeping me so closely in touch that, with the aid of
his daily diary which I read cover to cover on his
return, I had a detailed picture of what happened to
him and to Matthew.

The flight took them over the Atlantic, up over the
great lakelands which fill much of the Minnesota
countryside, to Rochester, a town famous for being
home to the Mayo Clinic. It was the first time Matthew
had flown, and he was too excited to be nervous. They
had arrived in such good time at Gatwick Airport that
there was about an hour to fill between checking in
and boarding. Matthew and Fred were taken through
some back corridors, up some escalators to the North-
west Orient VIP lounge where the air hostesses

showed him to a free bar and sat him down with some comics. Fred had a beer while Matthew had a Coke. They must have looked out of place among all the immaculately dressed business magnates who shared the VIP lounge: Fred in a cotton jersey shirt and casual trousers, and Matthew in slacks and blazer.

The ground staff had been told to make Matthew welcome and that he was 'disabled', so they repeatedly offered wheelchair assistance, or rides to the aeroplane in one of the little buggies usually seen on a golf course. All the suggestions, all the offers of help were completely inappropriate although kindly meant. Even on the plane, Matthew was asked if he wanted any help to move about; he proved that he didn't need any assistance by exploring the plane top to bottom, including the hallowed sanctuary of the galley where the air hostess got very sniffy about his intrusion. The first airline meal, the usual concoction of plastic lettuce and massacred chicken, delighted Matthew who saved all the tiny packets of pepper, salt and mustard, and the freshen-up pad. This was followed by hot flannels to revive him – he used them although they can't have helped his fast-drying skin. And then there were the films which meant that Matthew refused to have a nap during the flight. When there was nothing to eat or see inside the plane Matthew, who had insisted on a window seat, pressed his nose to the window to see what was going on outside, even if it was just the passing clouds below.

Halfway through the flight the captain invited Matthew to the cockpit. By this time he had already explored the plane so thoroughly that he was able to lead Fred, Jane Owen and David Graves through the main cabin, up the spiral staircase to the business class through to the cockpit where the three officers on duty gave every impression of never having to do anything. Matthew's eyes fixed on to the banks of dials and switches, lights and monitors, but before he could start to ask questions he was being asked to contort into various positions for David Graves, the *People* photographer. David wanted pictures of Matthew beside the captain, beside the joystick, looking out of the window and heaven only knows what, all in the confined space of the cockpit.

Matthew's first stop in the States was St Pauls, where he and Fred had a four-hour wait before transferring to a much smaller aircraft. Queuing was Matthew's first experience of the New World; queuing to talk to immigration officials, who were bounced out of their surly bureaucratic mode by their curiosity about Matthew. They sent him off with wishes of good luck – how unlike their British equivalents! The wait at St Pauls was filled in with a tour of the shopping arcades and cafés, with Matthew in the lead while the rest of the party dragged behind, tired by the long flight.

In Rochester they were met by a small official welcoming committee of local dignitaries, the local fire chief Orville Mertz and reporters from the local radio, television and newspapers. It had been a long, tiring flight but Matthew, as always, gave some excellent off-the-cuff interviews. He's not known as 'one-take' for nothing! It was mid-evening local time, so Matthew and Fred were taken straight to their host and hostess for the first week: Earl and Anna McGee. As soon as Bob Monk had alerted the fire-fighters in America to Matthew's arrival they decided he would feel more at home staying with a black family. So they contacted the leading black couple in Rochester, Earl and Anna, whose family had left home and who had become heavily involved in community work. They are kind, warm-hearted people who welcomed Fred and Matthew without reservation. Their house, in a prosperous, leafy suburb, became a second home. Earl is an excellent cook, specializing in barbecues. The second night that Fred and Matthew were there, Earl made a fabulous chicken dish over apple wood chips on the fire, while Anna produced an array of vegetables and salads. It was a feast, and already the weather was warm enough to sit outside well into the evening. It was a lovely way to start their stay in the States.

The following morning they had to buckle down to business and, still jet-lagged and dazed by a new place and the sudden heat, they had to spend most of the day filling out forms at the Mayo Clinic. Fred had to fix times and dates for all Matthew's medical tests, book a bed and arrange payment – yes, everyone usually has to pay for surgery before they are accepted into American hospitals, and Matthew was no exception. It was a far cry from the NHS but everyone was helpful in that 'have-a-nice-day' way. So many things seemed to have happened in those first few days that I don't know how Fred and Matthew managed.

Matthew had been asked by various dignitaries and organizations in Kent to take presents to sister organizations in Minnesota. He turned into an efficient ambassador for the country. The local fire service, well briefed by our friend Bob Monk in Kent, opened the fire station to Matthew and gave him an afternoon to play on their fire engines, ranging from an old one with glittering brass trim and fittings, and buckets down the side, to the newest model with all the latest fire-fighting equipment. They even let him ride in their old fire engine during a street carnival. After Fred and Matthew had been up on the vertigo-inspiring extending ladder – they showed me the pictures later and I was glad I hadn't been there – Matthew presented the fire chief with a Kentish fire-fighter's helmet and a plaque, and in return he was given a Minnesota fire-fighter's helmet for the Kentish firemen and some badges for himself.

But the craziest moment of that afternoon was a 'fire awareness' demonstration which involved a remote-controlled robotic fire hydrant. From one angle this fire hydrant looked perfectly normal: just like the type you see in films of New York, spouting water during the height of the summer. But then, without warning, Herbie the Hydrant would move off down the 'sidewalk' chatting to people. From the back Herbie looked ordinary, but from the front he had eyes and his voice came, by walkie-talkie, from anyone who happened to be in charge of his controls. It was a recipe for chaos in the streets as Herbie accosted passers-by to chat to them about the weather, their clothes – and, of course, fire safety. Matthew was allowed to have a go and used Herbie to chat up an extremely good-looking American girl.

Just as the fire-fighters had done, the Scouts organization of America gave Matthew some souvenirs, while he gave them a plaque, pennants and souvenir plates from Deal. It was only day two and yet Matthew was already a local celebrity. People had seen him on the television and in the local newspapers and so, when they saw him in the street, they would come up and say 'Hi', or want to shake his hand or just wish him luck. Matthew took everything in his stride and he answered questions about himself without appearing to be upset. Americans are so much more direct than English people, and they tend to ask some very probing personal questions as soon as they are introduced. In a way it seemed a better way of doing things: they were openly curious but rarely rude. They would ask Matthew directly what had happened to his face instead of waiting, as many English people do, to ask Fred or me. The only time anyone out there was deeply insensitive was on board one of the local planes when a snub-nosed, blond-haired all-American kid hollered, 'Hey, dad, look there's a monster getting on the plane.' If Matthew had noticed, he wasn't about to show it.

Perhaps Matthew's most prized discovery in those first few days was American ice-cream. The ice-creams served in the café of the hotel where Jane Owen and David Graves were staying had to be seen to be believed, with lots of different flavoured scoops, chocolate flakes, fudge topping, bananas, spinkles of nuts and cocktail umbrella all in one gigantic glass. The confection was bigger than Matthew's head and his stomach as he proved time and again by ordering one but eating only a fraction of it. He made up for that by nibbling all the time – half a hamburger, a few chips, a few sips of milk shake and ice-cream, mostly, although as always he never put on an ounce.

The hotel café was to become a regular haunt. It is connected to the main Mayo Clinic building by an underground tunnel, so it is like an extension of the hospital. Wheelchairs and bandages are a regular sight in the café as well as worried – or happy – looking relatives. Like the rest of this strange little community, the café focuses almost entirely on the clinic. It is as if all the shops, the restaurants and the hotels owe their custom to the clinic, the medical staff, the patients and the relatives of those at the Mayo: it is a highly polished, sophisticated urban centre in the midst of picturesque farming country, like a lush, tidy version of parts of Devon.

The day starts early at the clinic, and at half past seven on his third day in Minnesota Matthew was at his first appointment with Professor Ian Jackson, in the pristine square marble block which is home to the main part of the clinic. Matthew thought that the examination room looked like a dentist's surgery.

Matthew has extraordinary faith in all those around him, and he always quietly let things happen to him. But Fred noticed that he made frequent trips to the toilet, and that his eyes darted constantly from side to side, a sure sign that he was nervous. Professor Jackson is a tall, imposing man, over six feet, with pale brown, slightly greying hair. I should imagine he is in his fifties, though his face looks younger. His dress and appearance are modest, belying his whizz kid career: I have been told that he is regarded as a guru in his profession. He is a quietly spoken, reassuring man and you know as soon as you meet him that you can trust and confide in him. He is kind, down-to-earth and straightforward, and not nearly as aloof as some of the medical people that Fred and I have met. In his soft, Scottish accent he explained that Matthew would have to undergo a series of detailed tests, which would take about two days: never having come across Ablepheron Macrostomia Syndrome, on top of the fact that the medical world can pinpoint only one similar case – a boy who died in his early teens – Professor Jackson wanted as thorough an investigation of Matthew as possible. During that first meeting five other doctors were present, all representing different fields of medicine.

Professor Jackson asked Fred and Matthew what they wanted to achieve and slowly elicited a long list: eyelids that closed; a mouth that opened sufficiently and flexibly enough to be able to eat more easily (as proved by his appetite, Matthew's mouth size had never caused him insurmountable problems, but a larger one would make life easier) and smile, a luxury denied to him all his life; ears positioned so as to be able to support glasses; an end to constantly watering eyes; a moister skin so that it no longer cracked and bled so easily; an improvement in hair growth; any improvement to the nose, which was so tiny that it tended to block easily; the de-webbing and freeing of Matthew's fingers, which were bent in a fixed position; and various internal adjustments which would ensure his natural development. Above all, in Matthew's words, 'Please just let me look like everyone else'.

I'm sure the doctors had seen it all before, and worse, but their tact and concern impressed Matthew and Fred. What is more, they directed all their questions and suggestions to Matthew rather than Fred, unlike some of the doctors they had dealt with in the past. That was so much better; after all, Matthew was going to be on the receiving end of their treatment. He liked the doctors a lot, and was fascinated by their accents. No decision about treatment could be made until the test results came through. Matthew left the surgery with a four by six-inch beige folder which contained each day's appointment logged on separate cards showing time and date, and each was arranged to give just enough time to get from one appointment to the next: not as simple as it might sound, because the clinic is spread within a square mile or so of separate blocks.

The first day of tests began badly. Blood tests were needed and these more than surgery or any other test were what Matthew dreaded. It took two people to hold him down – Fred and a nurse. It was over in seconds but Matthew struggled and pulled his arm away and cried. We have this performance every time he has a blood test. Spread over two days, Matthew was given brain scans; head X-rays; a probing dental examination; kidney X-rays; a hearing test; a test on his skin, which involved taking a tiny scraping for microscopic examination to see if its condition could be improved; and eyesight tests. They even had a set of photographs taken of him from every angle. Matthew was taken to the hospital photographic studio which was filled with vast studio lights, silver photographic umbrellas and several cameras. The photographer asked him to stand at the centre of the room while she took pictures of his face, ears and hands from every angle with hand-held cameras and cameras on tripods. The hospital had thought of everything.

Except Matthew's appetite, that is, so Fred rejuggled some of the appointments to squeeze in an ice-cream break or two. Matthew and Fred came to the end of their second day of tests at five-thirty, when it was explained to them that his face would need a lot of rebuilding with bone and skin grafts to give him cheekbones before any work could begin to give him the ears he needed and wanted so badly. The acid imbalance in his skin which caused his eczema could not be cured, but it could be helped. There was so much surgery to be done, much more than we had expected, that Professor Jackson decided not to begin work on Matthew's hands during this trip. It sounded drastic. A lot of work was needed, but at least now we knew in some detail that Ian Jackson would be able to help, and that Matthew's dream might start to come true.

DISNEY WORLD

With Matthew away I could devote all my attention to the other children and show them how much I loved them to make up for the fact that Matthew had been the centre of attention for several months. We played endless card games to which only they appeared to know the rules, we played draughts so long as they won, I read them stories and bought them their favourite videos: Snoopy cartoons. But their favourite pastime was ringing Matthew. They would look forward to the calls for days. I would line up my higgledy-piggledy tribe and let them say hello to Matthew and Fred one by one. They loved it. Ben missed Matthew the most and I often found him asleep in Matthew's bed. 'I'm keeping it warm for him, mum,' he'd explain.

Although I missed Matthew and Fred a great deal I was coping very well. I'm an Indian, not a chief, and I'm good at keeping things going with the help of all our friends, who called or popped round daily to make sure I was all right. And Lorraine stayed with me, so I had all the moral and practical support I needed. Bob Monk, too, lent a hand whenever he could although I've no idea how he found the time, because he spread his energy and influence to both sides of the Atlantic. His ability to organize people and events at long distance is remarkable. He is a Mr Fixit, and his propaganda about Matthew inspired the Orlando fire-fighters in Florida to offer Fred and Matthew a few days' holiday there before the surgery began. But this was not any old holiday – they had arranged for Matthew to spend a day at Disney World and to visit Cape Canaveral.

Matthew was turning into a cool jet-setter. He was given VIP treatment on Northwest Orient, which meant use of their VIP lounges – comfy chairs, free coffee, drinks and snacks – and the privilege of having his luggage off-loaded before any other passenger so that he never had to wait for it. His cases were stowed beside the passenger door and carried off as soon as the doors were open. But it wasn't only the VIP treatment which made Matthew stand out as an air traveller. He had taken to this life with the ease of an old campaigner, slipping off into the airport lounge to buy himself a Coke or make a telephone call back home to me: 'American pay phones are much better than ours, mum, you can dial anywhere with a credit card,' he explained. He learned to read the departure boards and find his way around airports without help from Fred or any of the air hostesses who offered to escort him.

There was one stopover from Minnesota before Fred, Matthew and their personal press entourage of Jane Owen and David Graves arrived in Orlando to be met by a fleet of fire-fighting officials. The airport was cool and air-conditioned, but as soon as they set foot outside they were knocked backwards by the heat. It was that heavy, dry heat typical of the Everglades, which dries your skin in seconds. The fire-fighters loaded the baggage into their cars and took Matthew and his party to a brand new hotel on the edge of town. Sprinklers swished water across the newly-laid lawns and in the hotel entrance hall a fountain and series of cascades splashed through the centre of an

111

eight-storey-high rotunda. This was just the foyer, although you could hardly see the reception desk for the grand chrome and etched glass water sculpture surrounded by exotic plants at the centre.

Matthew was shown to his room on the fifth floor which overlooked a gigantic kidney-shaped swimming pool. It had two king-sized double beds, a colour television, an en suite bathroom packed with free bubble baths and soap and, to his utter delight, a telephone beside which there was a room service menu. He mastered this at once and, lying back on one of the beds, he button pushed his order for ice-cream, milk shake, hamburger, and all the trimmings, to room service while watching 'Batman' on cable television. Matthew was in his element.

Fred lured him downstairs, out of his room, only after a great deal of persuasion, and took him to explore the hotel complex. It was attached to a new, marble-floored shopping mall, so guests never had to go outside to find any of their creature comforts. There were clothes shops, soda fountains, souvenir shops, shoe shops and snack bars, and it was there that Matthew discovered a pair of sophisticated, aviator-style sunglasses made in such a way that he could wear them by hooking them into a baseball cap he had worn non-stop since buying it in Rochester. Fred bought them. They made life much easier for Matthew, because the bright Florida sunlight had made his eyes suffer and stream even more than usual. The baseball cap, glasses and a sweatshirt from the Harrington pub in Derby, which had raised so much money for him just a month or so earlier, became Matthew's favourite outfit. I think that one of the advantages of this outfit, from Matthew's point of view, was that the glasses and the large-peaked cap effectively covered his face, so he was less prone to stares from strangers.

112

Later, before the sun went down, Matthew, Fred and Jane swam in the pool. They were the only people there, and splashed about for an hour or so. Matthew was to discover yet another peak of luxury: being able to order drinks by the pool. The high life definitely suited him. And all this had been paid for and arranged by the Orlando fire-fighters, who had never had anything to do with Matthew or with our community in Kent: these were just good-hearted, generous men. Skip Lemay, one of the Orlando fire-fighters who was to become a friend and guide over the next few days, arrived at the hotel the following evening. Skip is a tall, gentle man who had an immediate affinity with Matthew, and right from the start never made any special fuss but treated him as he would have any kid. He suggested going out for a sort of Wild West evening of wine, women and song at an Orlando street festival. There were Dixieland jazz bands, chorus girls singing and dancing, plenty of beer, soft drinks and hamburgers, and a great big welcome for English people. Once again Matthew became an instant celebrity.

But the whole point of the visit was to see Disney World, and if it had been anything else I doubt if Matthew would have left his room for a whole day: he really loved the luxury of hotel life. Matthew was taken into Disney World in Skip's car, a gleaming limo with plush red velour inside, the likes of which Matthew had never before seen. The party was whisked round to the special VIP entrance, a bonus arranged through the fire-fighters; guided around the centre on monorail, boat and steam train; taken on a boat ride through swamps with such life-like crocodiles and elephants that even Matthew jumped a little. But his favourite 'ride' was the racing cars – miniature cars on a circuit – which he rode at least ten times, beating all the rest of the party.

The Epcot Centre was not so much of a success for Matthew. I think the slightly educational approach of some of the 'rides', showing how plants grow without any soil, or how crops are grown worldwide, was a bit off-putting for him after a day spent meeting a full-size Mickey Mouse amongst others. Fred enjoyed himself, though, because one dramatic show, in which the auditorium itself moved about, showed how coal and petrol come to be created, a subject dear to Fred's heart despite redundancy. But Matthew was tired, and he was beginning to miss his hotel room, his room service telephone and his television; Skip registered the danger signs and got him back before any whining set in. Matthew was so enamoured with the hotel that, when the following night Fred, Jane, David, Skip and his wife went out to dinner to eat crocodile steaks, Matthew insisted on staying behind to watch tele-vision from his bed and order a meal from room service. He was beginning to show just how indepen-dent he could be.

The following morning, though, Matthew was again one of the party when Skip arranged a trip to the Cape Canaveral space centre, an hour or so's drive away through scrub country and a nature reserve to the coast. Matthew was introduced to Cape Canaveral by a film about the history of space travel, dedicated to the astronauts who had died only recently in the Apollo explosion. Once again Skip was the guide for the day and, on the way out to the space centre, took Matthew to see his fire station, where Matthew and the fire chief exchanged gifts and souvenirs and the local Press interviewed him. That Sunday Skip took Matthew to a Catholic service near the hotel: he too was Catholic. It was an odd service, very much more informal than anything Matthew had been used to, and set in a modern church with the pews arranged amphitheatre-style around the altar. But, however odd the service, it was a fitting end to Matthew's break before surgery began.

In those few days, Skip had become the equivalent of an older brother/friend/father-figure, and so it was hard for Matthew to say goodbye to him and head back to the ordeal ahead. As always he didn't fret or complain, but lived life from one ice-cream to the next. Jane Owen and David Graves left Fred and Matthew at Orlando to fly back to the UK direct, while Fred and Matthew climbed aboard their plane for Minnesota. At least they were returning to friendly faces and a place they knew.

SURGERY

Two days on from the sumptuous luxury of his hotel room in Florida, Matthew was lying unconscious in the Mayo's intensive-care ward after his first operation in America. He was unrecognizable. Bandages covered the top half of his head, which had been cut open, leaving him in a world of complete darkness, unable to see because his eyes were covered and unable to hear much. Cartilage had been slipped into position where his ears would be, and unless you stood very close to him and spoke loudly he couldn't hear more than a muffled mumble.

In a post-anaesthetic haze of confusion and pain, Matthew didn't know what time of day it was; he would doze for three minutes and wake convinced he'd slept through the night and woken the following morning. Nurses sat silently beside him watching his drip and monitors, but Fred had to stay at his bedside for two days solid. The slightest movement woke him, and if Fred let go of Matthew's hand, even if Matthew was asleep, he would wake and beg Fred to stay. Two small drains, which looked like upturned test-tubes, were attached to either side of his head, each collecting blood which drained from his vestigial ears. A catheter and bag were attached to his lower half, and a stream of nurses kept constant watch on his blood pressure, pulse and temperature. Surgery had

116

started at seven o'clock in the morning on 3 June and had lasted for twelve hours.

As Fred told me about those first few hours after the initial operation, my spirits flagged: I knew we had done the right thing in letting Matthew go through with it, but if only he didn't have to suffer. He groaned and cried. Fred held his hand and talked to him, told him he was there beside him. It was all he could do. As Fred waited for Matthew to come round we had one of our longest telephone calls. He filled me in on everything that had happened, especially since Matthew had been admitted.

Matthew and Fred had arrived back in Rochester from Florida on Sunday night for the surgery to begin first thing on Monday morning. Fred and Matthew had to get to St Mary's hospital, which is part of the Mayo Clinic, at seven-thirty. Matthew was very nervous. He had a bath in the bathroom attached to his room and got into bed, only to be moved on to a trolley and wheeled to the theatre to meet his anaesthetist, who gave him a pre-med. Matthew chattered away nonsensically as the pre-med took hold of him. Fred just humoured him and reminded him that dad would be there when he woke up. He watched Matthew falling into drowsiness as he was wheeled away. And from then on, while Matthew was in surgery, Fred couldn't help in any way. He had no choice but to sit and wait.

The main point of this surgery was to change the shape of Matthew's face – he had an oversized forehead and an elf-sized chin – to a more balanced one which would accommodate more easily a 'proper' mouth and ears. The skin on Matthew's head was cut from above one ear hole, over the top of his head, down to the other ear hole, and then his face was literally peeled forward from the bone. Bone from either side of the skull was removed and grafted on to

117

his upper cheekbones. His old cauliflower ears were removed and the cartilage from those placed in his chest to preserve them until they were needed for his new ears. Then the skin was replaced and sewn back. That was followed by some major internal surgery to ensure Matthew's natural development.

At least Matthew would return from intensive care to his very own dad and to a clean, attractive room – even if it was hundreds of miles away from his home. It was a creamy-white room on the sixth floor of St Mary's hospital, overlooking the main street of the small north-west American town, where the café and souvenir shops huddle next to motels, all serving an international clientèle of patients attending the world-famous clinic. There were two single beds separated by a locker with a telephone on top. The other bed was empty. To one side of the room there was a small bathroom and toilet, and against the wall a colour television and a radio.

Matthew shared a shift-by-shift succession of nurses with five other children housed in nearby rooms and, as the shifts changed, Fred got to know them all on first-name terms, which is the American way of doing things. They were all attractive, well-groomed women, cheerful, kind, relaxed, and dressed in white trouser-suits or shift-style uniforms with white shoes – they make English nurses look old-fashioned. Down the corridor there was a playroom and a games room. Matthew's room could have become a games room in its own right: school friends back in England, new friends young and old made in America, and even complete strangers who had read Matthew's strange and courageous story, had sent him computer games, books, toys, puzzles and cards. I shall never know how Matthew gets to be so well-known and well-liked wherever he goes: cards addressed 'Courageous Matthew, Minnesota' would get to our Matthew.

His favourite toy was still Checky, the teddy he had brought from England, but since his arrival in the States he had been hankering after a brown furry toy monkey. He had spotted it in the shopping mall just before he went into hospital for the operation. He had loved it. 'It's cuddly and soft, just like dad's belly,' he said. Cheeky thing. Anyway, it was quite expensive but Fred bought it for him and arranged it on the hospital bed so that it would be the first thing he felt when he woke up. He just clung to it whenever the pain was bad, and even now it is his favourite toy – along with Checky.

Fred sounded so tense as he filled me in on what had been happening, and I wished there was some way I could help. He had no idea whether Matthew would be all right, or whether the surgery would be a success, he just had to wait and see. Fred tried to eat, only to find that he had lost his appetite. Knowing how little sleep he would be getting in the next few days when Matthew came round, Fred tried to sleep but dozed and woke so often that he decided instead to watch some television. He wasn't to return to Northlands, the hostel where they were staying, for three days. Matthew regained consciousness very soon after surgery, but he was too dopey and dazed to make much sense. After a few days, when the worst of the pain was over, Matthew became less clingy, so releasing Fred long enough to have a meal and pop back to Northlands. Two days later Matthew was allowed out of bed. His head was still heavily bandaged and he was still unable to see, so Fred and the nurses had to lead him around the room. It was emotionally draining for Fred as well as Matthew, who cried and fretted every time his dad wanted to go to Northlands for a rest.

Towards the end of the first week, Matthew began to show signs of getting back to his old self; he started complaining about hospital food and asking for ice-cream. But as the immediate concern about his pain and trauma eased away, the more longterm worry hung over us: had the surgery been a success?

One week after that operation a nurse arrived to remove some of the head bandages. She gently unwound them, bathing off some strips which had stuck to Matthew's head. Fred said it seemed to take an age but in fact it was about five minutes. Matthew's face was very swollen, so much so that Fred was reluctant to give him a mirror. But Matthew, who had been completely silent through the unbandaging apart from the occasional 'ouch!', insisted. He was taken aback by his appearance. He was very quiet, but even then I think he had such faith in Professor Ian Jackson that he didn't let himself worry unduly.

Fred, Matthew and the nurse waited for Professor Jackson, who arrived with another doctor to examine Matthew's head. They scrutinized it, touched it, and finally said they were delighted with the results. They also reassured Fred that the swelling would vanish within a week or so. The swelling was severe, giving Matthew's normally elfin face a strange, bulbous appearance, and I think that even with the Professor's reassurances, Fred was worried. But as far as the professionals were concerned everything had gone exactly to plan, except for one element of the operation. Matthew's eyes were causing great concern because they had swollen and the eyeballs themselves had developed blisters. There was never any danger to his eyesight, but his eyes were very sore. They were treated with eye drops and washes, but Matthew was in a lot of pain and had to wear a protective device, which looked like a pair of swimming goggles, to keep his eyes moist until the blisters healed. But for a long time after he was discharged, the surgeon checked Matthew's eyes every single day. Light hurt them so he had to wear sunglasses most of the time, even when he was in bed.

As the days wore on and the pain began to subside Matthew – still in bandages, like some half-awake mummy – started ringing his friends back home. Fred rang daily and increasingly he sounded bored and tired. Outside, the temperature hovered in the 100s and, even in the air-conditioned inside, the atmosphere was too heavy and humid for people who are used to the fresh sea air of Kent. Fred, Anna, Earl, their young friend Donald, and a succession of new-found friends in Rochester, read adventure stories like *Tom Sawyer* to Matthew, talked and entertained him as the routine of examinations, checks and drug times rolled by. There was our son, swathed in bandages, surrounded by people who were strangers to me, all because so many other strangers in Britain had decided to help give Matthew the surgery he wanted and needed so badly. The operation left Matthew tired as well as in pain even when he had been discharged from the hospital. He had to wear a catheter and bag for several weeks after his internal operation, and the apparatus gave him endless amusement. If he forgot to empty his bag and then lay down he would wet his bed, which Matthew thought very funny although the joke wore a bit thin on Fred. Matthew could never tell whether or not he had passed water because he had a catheter, and so he used to lift his dressing-gown, peer down at the bag strapped to his leg and proudly announce, 'I've been'.

On the day that Matthew was released he was told that he would have to return to hospital in seven days for further surgery. This was no surprise because we had been told that a follow-up operation on this trip was very likely. Fred tried to make that seven days away from institutional life a complete break for Matthew. He cooked their meals – nice homely food like sausages and bacon – or they ate out in little cafés dotted around the town. Matthew's appetite had returned quickly and he was soon tucking into his favourites: hamburgers, ice-cream and milk shakes. They watched Matthew's favourite videos, met up with a few of the fire-fighters and others who had first welcomed them to Rochester, and spent some days window-shopping. But they couldn't do that for any stretch of time because Matthew was still recovering: he couldn't walk far, so his outings were often limited to long car trips into the country. Whatever he did, he had the goodwill of the Rochester community behind him, and every time he left or went into hospital, every time he coughed, or so it seemed, the local newspaper reported it.

Northlands House meanwhile, the place and the people, had become a second home for Matthew and Fred. It had been bought by a trust fund set up by parents of children at the Mayo Clinic to give parents and their children somewhere homely, cheap and close to the clinic to stay during treatments. For many of the residents, the Mayo was their last hope and where they invested the last of their savings. Yet everyone, no matter what their own problems were, bolstered up everyone else and helped to make Northlands a real family home. The people at Northlands rarely have much to be happy about: their children have brain tumours, cancer and many dreadful diseases, and yet there is an atmosphere of hope, optimism and caring. You feel you will always have a friend at Northlands, perhaps because everyone there is in the same boat, everyone knows exactly how worried the other parents are and so they naturally give as much support as they can when they're up, and take as much support as they need when they are down. I was glad Fred was staying there because at least he had friendly faces around him.

Each family at Northlands has a room to itself, but the kitchen and television room is communal and so, almost every evening of their stay, Fred – and Matthew when he wasn't in hospital – would share a meal around the television with the rest of the families. Fred and Matthew earned star status by virtue of their accents – the rest of the Northlands inhabitants, all of whom were American, just *loved* an English accent and would ask Fred and Matthew to talk for entertainment's sake.

Even while Matthew was well enough to recuperate at Northlands, he had to have a check-up every day with Professor Jackson at the hospital. One day, while Fred and Matthew were waiting to see the Professor, his wife Marjorie appeared and sat with them for about fifteen minutes, asking how they were enjoying America and asking after me because the only contact she had had with our family was through my letters. She left saying she would like Matthew to come to her house to meet David – so-called 'Boy David' – their adopted son whose televised story had sparked off Matthew's adventure. That day, on top of all the regular checks on Matthew, Professor Jackson ran through a series of tests on his skin. He said it would be fine for Matthew to swim, so he should bring his trunks when he met Boy David and they could swim together in the Jacksons' pool. Fred jumped at the chance of meeting the family and of giving Matthew the opportunity to meet someone with such similar experiences.

After a light lunch Fred and Matthew packed up their towels and killed a little time by driving along a scenic route to the Jacksons' home. Their house is set in lush deciduous woodland, a hundred yards or so from the main road down a private drive. The homestead is a brown clapperboard bungalow which spreads across a clearing in the trees to a swimming pool, where David and his brother were playing. As Fred and Matthew's car scrunched up the drive the two boys came to meet them. Within five minutes Matthew had changed and flopped into the pool with them. They took charge of a rubber boat and began taking turns to paddle up and down the pool or knock each other out of the boat. They looked as if they had known each other for years. Marjorie and Fred sat on the terrace overlooking the pool and chatted about the boys.

After a while the boys tired of swimming and started to play American football, of a kind, which eventually became a competition to see who could throw and catch the best. It was a little unfair because of Matthew's trigger-fingered hands and his inexperience, but he didn't seem to mind losing. Fred doesn't think that Matthew and David, both then aged about twelve, ever talked about their experience of surgery or of adoption, they simply enjoyed each other's company for the afternoon. But although they never discussed these things the meeting appeared to make Matthew more relaxed and happy than he had been since his arrival in the States.

Earl and Anna still played second mum and dad to Matthew – and to Fred – inviting them for meals, and visiting them regularly at Northlands and at the hospital. And during Matthew's week away from hospital, Earl and Anna came up trumps by throwing open their house for Matthew and Fred to visit as and when they wanted, and arranging all kinds of outings and special meals. Matthew loved all their cooking, especially some of their creamy cakes, their sweets, fruit and their special barbecued chicken. This time, Matthew was more relaxed about going into hospital. And he was buoyed up by the prospect of having eyelids that worked. Apart from the luxury of being able to close his eyes when he went to sleep, it would mean that he would be able to wink, or so he hoped, which was something he had never been able to do. Fred booked Matthew into the hospital the day before surgery was due to begin so that bills could be settled beforehand. This time Matthew was back in his old room, but with a room-mate called Ben. Just like home! Ben was seven years old, and came from a local farm. He was recovering from a broken arm, and he was in too much pain to get to know Matthew very well. But Ben's parents were very concerned about Matthew. They were kind, gentle people and asked Matthew and Fred to come to stay. So far they haven't taken up the invitation simply because there hasn't been time!

Matthew had to be at the hospital at seven in the morning for his second major operation in the States, and this time he was more relaxed about the system. He didn't even have to see Professor Jackson before he went into theatre because the surgeon had seen Matthew the day before. This time surgery would take skin from Matthew's chest for his eyelids so that, apart from working properly, they would look more like normal lids – his first pair were a much darker colour than the rest of his face, giving him a slightly panda-like appearance. Also, a few slithers of bone would be taken from his hips to be put under his eyes.

The operation lasted for four hours, and once again Matthew had to spend a day in intensive care. Fred was allowed into the small ward, where two to three patients were connected to monitors and cared for by a large, experienced medical team. Matthew, who was still dopey from the anaesthetic, wasn't really aware that Fred was with him. When Matthew was wheeled back to his room he was in a slightly better position than after the first operation because he could hear. Therefore, although he couldn't see because his eyes were bandaged, he felt less frightened. All the same, he was still as clingy and demanding as he always is after surgery.

Once again Fred became chief story-reader, although he was never quite sure how much of any given story Matthew had heard because sometimes he would begin to snore halfway through. It was a difficult time for Fred. The novelty of being in America had worn off, and he had to cope with the worry of Matthew's operations single-handed. I think he quite naturally missed the family, England and me. And in a way it was a lonely time for him because, however kind and welcoming people like Earl and Anna were to him and Matthew, they could never be the same as real family. But every time Fred started to get a bit down in the dumps, a child's courage would bring him back to earth. There was one American kid, about the same age as Matthew, who was in the hospital to have a leg amputated because it was cancerous. And yet the child used to lie there in bed worrying about Matthew's problems. Luckily, there was nothing to worry about during Matthew's second operation, which was completed without a hitch. Matthew was back in Northlands House a week later.

Fred again threw himself into entertaining Matthew to take his mind off the pain as his body healed from surgery. There were more car trips and endless visits to Anna and Earl. By the end of the week Professor Jackson was so delighted with the way that Matthew had healed that he offered Fred and Matthew a choice: to return in September for further surgery or to stay on for a third operation there and then. It was a tough choice. On the one hand, it would have been good to get as much surgery out of the way as possible so that it wasn't hanging over Matthew. On the other, Fred had noticed that Matthew was becoming increasingly homesick, although he never said anything and never complained. I had detected a touch of homesickness in some of Matthew's phone calls, but I had to leave the final decision to Matthew and Fred. Three days after we had first discussed the possibility of Fred and Matthew returning, Fred rang. He sounded happier and more excited than I'd heard him since he first told me the news that Professor Jackson could help Matthew: he and Matthew had decided to come home. The children were ecstatic; there wasn't much sleep that night. I spent the evening ringing round our friends to tell them the good news.

Over the previous seven weeks we had got into such a routine of telephoning each other, and of my bringing all Matthew's friends round to the house to cheer him up by phone when he was especially homesick, that I hardly knew how we'd get back to normal. And would I like the new Matthew? Would his personality have changed as well as his appearance? Would he have become Americanized?

Meanwhile, Matthew had more important things on his mind than his family back home! As a local celebrity, and one who would be returning in September for further surgery, Matthew had many goodbyes to say and so that last week was packed. After saying goodbye to Earl and Anna and the local fire-fighters, and giving them all ornate china plates from Deal, Matthew toured the local shops to buy presents for his friends and family. There were American model cars for Simon and Ben, a doll for Lucy, a tape of a completely unheard-of rock band for Eddie, and a beautiful china clown for me which is sitting in front of me on my dressing-table as I write.

THE SMILE

There was a fleeting moment at Gatwick Airport
when, with Matthew standing right in front of me, I
didn't want to look at him, I didn't want to see how he
had changed. One of the television reporters was
asking me something, I don't know what, though,
because my legs and my mind had turned to jelly. But
suddenly I was hugging my Matthew. It was seven-
thirty in the morning and his arrival was causing
mayhem in one of the main concourses of the airport,
but I didn't care – Matthew was home and that was
what mattered. The television cameras, the flash-guns
of the Press cameras, the curious stares from passers-
by, the efficient airport staff trying to move our party
into a more discreet part of the airport, all faded into
oblivion as I kissed him and then stood back for a
moment to have a look at him.

Fred had sent me pictures of Matthew but they had
been taken so soon after surgery that it was difficult to
see what had changed permanently in his face and
what was only temporary. But there he was, taller, or
so it seemed, with a round face which somehow
looked more grown-up. And there was one major
surprise – a smile! Matthew had long dreamed of
smiling and here he was beaming away, though still
not in a way that you or I might smile because lip

surgery had not yet been started. But his cheekbones had been built up in such a way that he was able to give a kind of smile.

Matthew was tired and a bit overawed by the Press. He was used to media attention, but this time there were so many, including two national television crews. Stranger still, he was a little shy of me. But I knew that as soon as he was back home and we were alone together he would open up. Suddenly, Fred's arms were around me and I heard him saying, 'We're back, love.'

With the help of Bob Monk, who had driven us to the airport while Lorraine played mum back home, we picked up the baggage as we talked to reporters and forged our way to the car park. We were greeted in Deal by a TVS camera team standing in our road! Philip Hornby from TVS, who had followed Matthew's story from the early days, was there to meet us and interview Matthew. But no sooner did Matthew start talking than Zoe, Lorraine's daughter and our granddaughter, who was becoming a little blonde bombshell and quite an extrovert, opened the front door and let out the two dogs, who bounded across to meet us, followed by Lorraine herself. There were tears of happiness then and later at four o'clock when the children arrived back from school. The children were followed by a stream of friends and neighbours, and, although Fred and Matthew must have been exhausted, their excitement seemed to keep them going.

Finally, when all the Press had left, we made tea with sandwiches, cakes and biscuits: good old English tea to welcome back Fred and Matthew. For once there was no rush – everybody was too busy hugging and kissing everybody else. Fred hardly had time to sip his tea between the hugs of all the children, who were determined to remind him that he was back where he belonged. Over tea Matthew gave us his presents, which led to even more chaos as the children played with their new toys.

Perhaps the only thing that spoiled the homecoming was the reaction of some friends and neighbours who simply did not understand how plastic surgery works. I suppose they thought Matthew would return with a completely transformed face without a suggestion of any deformity; perhaps they thought that he could be given a new face in the same way that you can pull on a mask. Of course, it isn't like that. It's a gradual process rather like building a model. You start with a framework and then start building on that, layer by layer. Between operations, as the body heals, the patient may even look worse than when the work started. But people don't always realize that. They expect an overnight miracle and their disappointment showed in their expression when they saw Matthew.

People have become so used to seeing television characters emerge completely unblemished after an accident or major plastic surgery that they seem to expect the same thing in real life. Television heroes who need plastic surgery seem to go into hospital with one face, to spend a few weeks talking through bandages and then to emerge looking completely different. Life may be like that in soap operas but, unfortunately, it is not like that in reality. Plastic surgery leaves bruising, swelling and scars. Sometimes Matthew's face looked a lot worse after surgery than it had before; and, even when the swelling subsided, the change was not immediately apparent to anyone but me, Fred and those who know him very well. We were well aware of this problem and, on top of explaining to Matthew again and again that there was no miracle cure, that changes would never happen overnight, we kept a video of the Boy David documentary by Desmond Wilcox and showed it to him several times. The documentary revealed the painstaking nature of the process, it showed David straight after surgery when his face was terribly puffed and unrecognizable, and it helped Matthew understand what was involved. His expectations of Ian Jackson's work have never been dashed, partly because we had been so careful to make him understand the point that many other people failed to grasp: plastic surgery is not a magic trick, not an instant solution.

I don't think that Matthew was troubled by other people's apparent disappointment in his appearance. For one thing he was too excited about being back home with all his friends and family. For another, he knew what was involved in plastic surgery and had every faith in his surgeon, Professor Ian Jackson. In fact, it was Matthew's new-found confidence which I thought one of the most striking changes in him.

As we packed the children off to bed, Lorraine said that TVam had rung to ask if Matthew would appear. Jet-lagged though they were, Matthew and Fred agreed, and the following day they took the evening train to Victoria where they were met by a TVam car and driven to an hotel near Lord's cricket ground for the night. They were woken at some unearthly hour to be in the Camden Lock studio at seven o'clock. There was the usual round of make-up girls and studio producers telling them what to expect, and then they were asked to wait in a small room just off the main studio where they were given coffee, orange juice and the daily papers.

The only other person in the room was none other than the real JR, Terry Trippett, the man who owns Southfork in real life; he was due to be interviewed in the slot before Fred and Matthew. Fred and Matthew were led into the large main TVam studio after a commercial break, and given a final dusting of powder to stop their faces shining in the bright studio lights. At last, at just after the eight o'clock news, Anne Diamond interviewed Matthew. 'One-take' Matthew did very well, and back in Kent, with the family gathered around the television, there was complete silence as we watched our Matthew telling Anne Diamond about his adventures and heard her saying how brave she thought he was. As the interview finished we clapped, while Matthew, who was the toast of the studio, was shown around. He seized the chance to collect more autographs for his book: Anne Diamond signed his book, and so did Wincey the weather girl and Nick Owen. He'd started the autograph book at the beginning of fund-raising so that he could keep a souvenir of all the people, famous and not-so-famous, who had helped him. He's got quite a collection of names, including that of Bob Champion who is one of Matthew's special heroes. Later, as Fred and Matthew were leaving Camden Lock, Terry Trippett appeared and gave Matthew his own South-fork brass belt buckle and an invitation to stay at the ranch whenever he wanted. Eat your heart out Cliff Barnes!

As the excitement about America began to die down Christine Piff, the founder of 'Let's Face It' and one of those who had been an especially close confidante during the seven weeks that Fred and Matthew were away, rang to suggest a new project for Matthew. Several years before, she had undergone major plastic surgery after cancer of the face and had discovered that there was no emotional support system to turn to. So she started an organization called 'Let's Face It' to help all those who have severe facial deformity, and to help and support their families. Matthew and I met Christine a year or so after she had started 'Let's Face It'. Now, to consolidate her organization's work, she was planning a documentary for

Channel 4 about the problems of facial disfigurement, and she wanted Matthew, who was then the only child in her group, to be on the programme. Would he agree?

I had come to respect and trust Christine a great deal while Matthew was away. It was Christine who reassured me and helped me through my moments of doubt, when I sincerely wondered whether we should have let Matthew go so far away from home to have such traumatic surgery. I knew that if she were in charge of the programme it would be responsible and balanced, so I talked to Fred about it and together we asked Matthew if he would like to do it. Without hesitation he said yes. Only a year ago he had hated showing his face – and yet here he was, confident and no longer ashamed of his appearance. It wasn't only that his appearance had changed; he had grown up emotionally and decided to look the world straight in the face.

Matthew's part in the documentary boiled down to about three solid days of filming, during which time our living-room looked like the aftermath of a battle in a spaghetti factory. Wires went everywhere, curling through windows from power packs outside, from all our power points, around sofas, through gaps in chairs, over tables. The crew had arrived in an assortment of cars and vans, so even the street outside looked odd. There were so many of them that I lost count. The lighting men erected powerful arch lights and various reflector boards around the room; the sound men fixed microphones to each of us and arranged a mobile boom overhead; the make-up artist dabbed a little powder on our faces to prevent shiny noses; the director and his assistant explained what would happen and what they would like us to do. There was even one assistant who spent a day arranging flowers around the room! Now, every time I see a neat little programme with three or four people talking to each other at someone's home, I think of those days making the documentary and laugh – the programmes always look so calm and yet, to make them, chaos reigns. Chaos also reigns just off camera and before and after each section of film that finally appears on our televisions at home. It was an education.

Oliver Gillie, the medical editor of the *Independent*, interviewed Matthew – or perhaps Matthew interviewed him. Matthew wanted to know about the large red mark, a port wine stain, on Oliver's face; Oliver wanted to know about Matthew's face. The interview worked very well. Matthew liked Oliver and opened up to him to a greater extent than he usually does.

As the last cameraman packed up and left our house our life began to get back to something like normality. We had had a year of a kind of stardom, of constant disruption of a sort we'd never expected. Now, for the first time, the media had lost interest in us and so we could buckle down to family life. Matthew went back to school a few weeks after he came home from the States, and Fred and I started to get to know each other again after a year spent being everyone else's property but each other's.

BACK IN THE USA

I am not a good traveller. I get carsick and I am scared of flying. My most enduring memory of flying, when I went to Germany with my parents as a child, was that of looking out of the window and seeing, to my horror, that the clouds were below me. I was not impressed and I didn't think that flying today would be much different, apart from the fact that we would be in a jet as opposed to a propeller-driven plane. If you are scared of flying, that kind of detail doesn't make much difference, but when it came to Matthew going back to America for further surgery I was determined to go. So was Matthew, who had announced that he would not go back without me.

Professor Ian Jackson had said he wanted to see Matthew again in September before winter when the temperature can dip to 40 below freezing. That would have hurt Matthew's sensitive skin even if he had put his head outside for just a few minutes. While we were in the States – and once again we did not know how long we would be there – the children would go to a holiday home, Beaver Lodge in Ashford, which is run by the local area health authority to give parents of handicapped children a much-needed break every now and then. The children loved it there and, because they went almost every year, they knew all the staff on first-name terms. In fact, the staff had become a sort of extended family to us. For two glorious weeks the children would be spoiled rotten. They would go to the zoo and to films and to local parks and swimming pools, and when one of them got a little homesick they could always ring us.

Normally Fred and I drove the children to Beaver Lodge, but this time we were so busy with arrangements for our trip to America that a local authority bus came to pick them up. Matthew helped his brothers and sisters pack – he does a lot for them one way and another. Each had to have three complete changes: three pairs of trousers, three pairs of pants, three jumpers, three dresses, three lots of everything. Then there were nappies, favourite teddies, special books and dolls, and everything else to prevent riot from the Learoyd children. This time Ben took Checky the teddy with him instead of letting Matthew take it. Matthew took his furry friend from his last lot of surgery, the large, cuddly monkey that had been on his pillow when he came round from the anaesthetic.

Matthew was very excited about going back to the States and, although he would once again have to face surgery, he managed to put that to the back of his mind while he concentrated on the thought of seeing all his friends again. Bob Monk and his daughter drove us to the airport and we arrived there to find, yet again, that Matthew's departure was causing a great stir. The local and national Press, radio and television had turned out to interview all three of us at Gatwick before we set off. Matthew smooth-talked his way through every interview, but ITN insisted on filming and refilming us checking in until they felt they had got it right. I am the type of person who would prefer to be swallowed up by the ground rather than appear on television, and I was very conscious of everyone's stares as we were being filmed. But Fred and I managed to say a few words and, although we would never make a living at it, I don't suppose we were too bad. What a relief, though, to get into the VIP lounge for a little peace and quiet. It was quite a change for me, too, to have people waiting on me hand and foot!

We sat on the top deck of the plane in executive class, which meant climbing spiral stairs away from all the smoke and bustle of the main part of the aircraft. There was much more room and much less chance of Matthew's eyes being irritated by cigarette smoke. Matthew was blasé about the adventure, showing us about the plane, explaining things to us like the seasoned traveller he had become. The food wasn't exactly my idea of breakfast or lunch but I wasn't able to eat anything anyway – too nervous – so I kept going on black coffee. Nine hours and one transfer later we were being met in Rochester, at lunchtime local time, by a fire-fighter called Joe Guyse and his wife, Jean, who had met Matthew and Fred on their last visit. They lived in a bungalow just outside Rochester, on the edge of rolling woodland typical of the uncultivated land around there, and they had agreed to pick us up because Joe had a day off.

I couldn't take anything in; I was overpowered by the heat. It was quite unlike anything I have experienced – a powerful, dry, overwhelming heat. Joe and Jean drove us around to show me a few of the landmarks which I had only ever heard about from Fred and Matthew. But I couldn't concentrate and the only thing I noticed was the size of the place. Everything seemed so vast – the landscape which dipped away into the distance in a way the English countryside never does, the skies which went on and on, and even the streets were so much wider and more airy than any British streets I have seen.

Peggy, the manageress of Northlands House, was overjoyed to welcome back Fred and Matthew, and told them that two of the families who had been there during their first visit were there again, too. Our room had two single beds and a mattress on the floor for Matthew. It was small, clean and tidy, and very homely. All I could think about was the prospect of getting into bed for a nice, long sleep. Matthew slept, too, long and deeply, and when he woke after about twelve hours solid we went to visit Earl and Anna, who turned out to be exactly as I had imagined them from all Matthew and Fred's letters and telephone calls about them. Earl and Fred cracked a few beers together while Anna and I drank coffee and talked. Matthew played cards with Earl, who still let him win every time.

I felt I knew Rochester and the clinic already because I had heard and read so much about them. So it was strange to see it all in the flesh for the first time. Everything was even grander and larger and more sophisticated than I had imagined. You could sense that this was the town where the Rockefellers and the US presidents came for treatment.

We had arrived on 1 September, and three days later we took the lift to the sixth floor of the Mayo main building to see Professor Ian Jackson, whom I remembered vividly from the 'Boy David' documentary. After a thorough examination of Matthew – a thoroughness which I came to realize was typical of this talented man – he said that he wasn't satisfied with the left-hand side of his head because the skull had sunk around the temple after the first operation. It was a tiny detail but Professor Jackson is a perfectionist. He explained that he would take further slithers of bone from Matthew's hip and graft them on to the left-hand side of his head to match it up with the right temple, and under the eye sockets to smooth and shape the existing holes. He also wanted to replace the lower lids and round the end of his nose. But the surgery which was dearest to Matthew's heart was the start of the work to give him a pair of working ears. This time, Ian Jackson wanted to take the cartilage stored in Matthew's chest from the previous surgery and to start building it into ear shapes *in situ*.

There was another round of extensive checks to make sure that nothing had been overlooked and that nothing had changed since the last series of operations. It was a gruelling schedule; we rushed from one part of the hospital to the next, squeezing in meal, coffee and cigarette breaks where and when we could. Poor old Matthew once more had to face blood tests, but he managed well this time. He didn't struggle or cry, he just clung to Fred's arm.

In the evenings, after Matthew and the rest of the children had gone to bed, we could switch off and relax with the rest of the parents. They were fascinated by us just because we were English, and they cross-questioned us about everything including the Royal Family. I was astonished at how little I knew about my own country and at how few questions about 'Lil' old England' I could answer. My knowledge of English history begins and ends with 1066 and all that. Theirs was considerably more extensive.

Matthew wanted to show me everything, to introduce me to the world he had discovered without my help. And so after the second day, which was taken up with medical tests, we set off into the town to explore the shopping malls and shops and hotels – and of course the ice-cream café, where we stopped off for one of Matthew's favourite concoctions, quite simply a glass filled with as many disparate flavours as could be squeezed in. We spent the evening at Earl and Anna's house and had a lovely meal.

Matthew was due to go into the operating theatre at seven o'clock the following morning, so we didn't stay out late. After a quick cup of coffee in the morning, we set off for the clinic. Matthew was brimming with confidence, striding ahead of us and explaining all the procedures to me as we went. He is so brave. I'll never forget his smiling face as he was wheeled away to the operating theatre by the anaesthetist. The hospital contacted us at Northlands House six hours later to say that the operation had been a success and that Matthew was in intensive care. We visited him but he was unconscious, and we were told that it was unlikely he would wake until the following day.

For the next three days Matthew cried, slept and hardly ate. But on the fourth day he began to perk up – he demanded ice-cream. There was a minor problem with one of his ears, which wouldn't stop bleeding, but that was easy to put right. His lower lids had been replaced and so bandages covered his eyes; he had had more work on his ears, which were also covered in bandages. Once again he couldn't see anything and he could hear only if we shouted. Fred and I spent the first few days after surgery shouting stories to Matthew as he lay recovering. Gradually he began to move about with the other children in the playroom. He couldn't join in because he couldn't see or hear much, so it was a case of describing to Matthew what the other children were doing. They were long-drawn-out days which seemed to go on for ever.

The monotony was broken one day by Professor Jackson's wife Marjorie, who popped in unexpectedly to see Matthew. She had brought David in for a minor operation and had called in to say hello while he was in surgery. I was disappointed that there was so little time to talk after all the letters we had exchanged. Marjorie was just how I had imagined her – energetic, easy-going and very kind. I wanted to ask her all the things that mothers always worry about, especially if their children are like Matthew or David: Did she worry about David's future? Did she think life for him was easier in the States or in her native Scotland? What did she think would happen to David when he left school and the protective circle of his school friends and family? What did she imagine David would do about girlfriends? But there wasn't time during her flying visit, so we have promised each other to talk about our sons some time in the future.

Visits from people like Marjorie always cheered Matthew up, but when there were no visitors to help while away the time Matthew's favourite pastime, as soon as his eye bandages came off, was to go up to the hospital roof garden to play in the open air and watch the helicopters bringing in patients from all over the States. It was a relief to break the monotony of staying in the same old hospital room day-in-, day-out, and it was wonderful to be in the open air, although the sun was so fierce that Matthew had to stay in the shade of the trees growing in tubs on the roof garden. Unlike the first operation, when Fred couldn't leave Matthew's bedside, Matthew felt so much more at home that we could leave him each night after he had gone to sleep. We were then able to get some sleep ourselves at the hostel. From there I would ring home every evening to talk to Lorraine and catch up on the news back home. I was so glad to be with Matthew and Fred, but I missed the rest of the family dreadfully.

Matthew recovered much faster from this operation than from the first two and after seven days he was discharged, although he was expected to rest up at Northlands and visit the surgeon every day until he had recuperated completely. Even by Matthew's standards he had made a swift recovery, and Fred told me that Matthew was in considerably better shape then, while I was with him, than he had been during his first visit, a few months earlier. A week later Professor Jackson announced that Matthew could return home that Saturday, which meant we would be home on the Sunday. I rushed back to the hostel and phoned Lorraine to tell her we were coming back that Sunday. She said she would arrange for the children to be returned home on the Monday.

There is still a lot of work to be done on Matthew before he can begin to feel comfortable and before his hands and face work as well as he would like them to. In a sense it is up to him to say when he feels right, when he feels surgery should stop, because most of the crucial work concerned with his long-term development has been completed.

Thanks to the trust fund, Matthew will always have the choice. The trust fund is well cared for by the trustees and, although Fred, Matthew and I rarely see them because we are not trustees ourselves and so cannot go to any of their meetings, we keep in touch by telephone. Today we rarely deal with the trustees face to face because most of them are based in Kent, and we are now living in our new home in Wales. But the routine remains the same wherever we live and wherever Matthew has to be sent for treatment. Once we know where and when Matthew is due for surgery, we ring one of the trustees to give him all the details. The trustees then hold a meeting, make the travel arrangements, pay for train, plane and taxi tickets in advance as far as possible, and put aside an allowance for whichever one of us is going to travel with Matthew. If the surgery involves going to the States, the trustees issue us with credit cards, just in case. For shorter trips in England for one of Matthew's check-ups, Fred normally does all the driving and takes care of the travel arrangements, but before he can claim any expenses back – from petrol money to meals on the journey – he has to submit detailed expense forms and receipts to the trustees who then reimburse him.

Sometimes it can be irritating at the end of a long day

to have to note down all those little extras that we have had to spend for Matthew's treatment; but of course in the long run it means that there can be no mistakes and no comebacks. We are all very conscious of the responsibility we have to use this money from the public as carefully as we can. That is one of the reasons why a formalized trust fund is crucial; it means that we have an independent body caring for the money so that the trust fund management can be seen to be fair and square.

The trustees will continue to look after Matthew's fund so that as he gets older and outgrows some of the surgery, and as new techniques appear, he may – or may not – decide to have more work done on himself. The important thing is that the choice is there for him to make, regardless of cost.

MERRY-GO-ROUND

Six months on from that bout of surgery began what I can only describe as the worst period of our family's life. It was eight months of sheer hell and, even now as I write about it, the memory makes me feel tearful. Matthew had fully recovered from his operation and was back at school, and we were back to normal. Once again our family was about to grow. Susan is a fifteen-year-old severely mentally handicapped child, tall, black, and completely unable to speak. We were asked to take her as a short-term foster child and, although we thought her a strange child, there was something about her that we liked, so we agreed.

Our children eyed her with curiosity. She never moved unless she was asked to, and she rarely made a sound. This is an unusual combination in our household. As the weeks passed and no more permanent place was found for Susan it became clear to us that she would be staying, probably for ever, as part of the family. She had learned to make a little grunting noise which stood for hello, goodbye, please, anything really. She had a terrible temper and sometimes flew into rages for no apparent reason, hitting out at anyone who happened to be in her way. She is bigger and a lot stronger than me, and she has knocked me to the ground more than once. But all the same, she had a special quality about her and we weren't about to throw her out. So now there were two dogs, the two of us and seven children: as much as we loved our little house it was time to move to a larger place. Our careful scrimping and saving since Fred's redundancy had bought us our council house on a mortgage, so now it was up to us, not the council, to find a new place. The house prices in Deal were too high for us so we started looking further down the coast and finally found a property in Margate.

19 March, 1987 is a date I will regret for the rest of my life. It was the day we moved. The children were great. They knew we were worried about the move and did their best to pack up their own bits and pieces, and encourage us to look forward to our new life. The trauma of moving is bad enough, but at least the children wouldn't have to change schools. As I said goodbye to all our kind friends and neighbours in Deal, I cheered myself up with the thought that they weren't too far away.

But from day one it was made clear by a few people in our new community that children like ours were not welcome. There were some who were kind and tried to help us, but most of them snubbed us, complained about our children's odd appearances, complained about our children's presence, complained about the odd noises they sometimes made, complained about the fact that some of them sometimes dribble and can't coordinate properly their movements.

Untold hurt was heaped on us. The children were called names if they went for a walk. Even when they played in the garden, some people complained that they were too noisy. The children didn't understand what was happening, they didn't understand why they weren't loved. They loved all those around them, so why didn't those around them feel love, too? The equation seemed so simple to them. Matthew never complained although he was clearly shocked and frightened by the reaction he and his brothers and sisters had received. He withdrew inside himself, buttoning up his feelings and refusing to talk much. He would disappear upstairs with Ben to play Lego, or they would sit watching television for hours on end. He seemed to adopt a self-imposed curfew, never going out unless he absolutely had to; his boisterousness, curiosity and energy faded and his school work took a nose dive. 'Why are other people allowed to have their radios and televisions on full blast, while we aren't allowed to play in the garden or have the television on loud?' he would ask.

Eddie withdrew into himself, stayed in his room almost all the time and reverted to bed-wetting. Lucy settled in well, oblivious to the tension, but Ben became very demanding and Simon started throwing many more violent temper tantrums than he had for several years. His back would arch backwards into a rigid frame, he would beat his head against the wall, or slap his head, and scream. Simultaneously, Sarah began to show a side of her nature which was increasingly impossible to deal with. She displayed traits which we could not control: she would starve herself for days at a time, refusing to eat or even drink a thing. But if she was self-destructive she was also destructive to us, and there seemed to be no way of changing that. She would refuse to talk to the other children, or she would become angry and unreasonable with them. Sometimes she would become physically violent, hitting out at me and the children.

Even Gemma my lovely Old English sheepdog suffered because of Sarah. Frustrated by having to spend so much time indoors, Sarah began to torment poor Gemma, and then encouraged Simon to do the same. All Gemma wanted was a nice, peaceful time. She is the soppiest dog I know and always insisted on

146

sitting on my lap, although she was far from a suitable size. When I discovered the children teasing Gemma, pulling her tail and pushing her over sideways I gave them a fierce telling-off and expected that to be an end of it. It wasn't. A couple of days later I discovered them doing the same, but this time Gemma was beginning to retaliate with a few little snaps. She was such a gentle creature that she had not yet actually bitten the children but I could see that it was only a matter of time. I loved the dog but the children's safety had to come first, and so I contacted the Old English sheepdog rescue service through the RSPCA and they arrived to meet Gemma and take her to a new home. They promised to find a good home for her where there were no children. Her departure was one more blow to my fast-sinking morale.

Sarah, meanwhile, continued to wreak havoc in the household. Without Gemma to tease she turned her attention to the other children and once reduced Matthew to tears. Since returning from the States, Matthew had taken it upon himself to lay the breakfast table every morning. Several mornings that March, as the family began breakfast, Sarah came in late, looked around and stormed out. Every time it happened, I went to her room to find out what was the matter and she told me she felt no one at the table wanted her there. It upset Matthew because he felt he was in some way responsible, which certainly wasn't true. It wasn't anybody's fault, it was just the way she reacts. But it was that kind of upset, and one or two violent incidents, which began to wear us all down.

We had had ten years of occasional violence and bad temper, mixed with moments of love and tenderness when Sarah would say how much she loved us and how much she wanted to live with us for ever. But as Sarah had grown – she was now twenty-one – so too had her problems and it was clear we could no longer look after her. It was heart-breaking but we decided she would have to live in a home outside the family. We found her one in Ramsgate, but we made it very clear to her that we had not rejected her and that she would always be a part of the family. She still comes to stay regularly and we phone each other every week. Three days after she left I sat down and wept for her. She had been with us for ten years and finally she had to go. It had taken that long for us to realize that Sarah needed us on her terms, not on ours.

Everything had gone wrong from the moment we moved into that house. I lost a stone in weight and a great deal of confidence. The final straw came one morning when there was a ring on the front door from a man from the local council. He was polite and straightforward: he had been told we were running an illegal children's home without any planning permission, and he had come to close us down. Fighting back the tears, I invited him in, gave him some coffee and asked him if he knew what adoption and fostering meant. He said he did. I explained our family set-up: some of the children were adopted and those who were fostered did not need planning permission! The council man's face fell as he heard my explanation, and the apologies came tumbling out. I felt sorry for him, he was only doing his job and he had been given misleading information.

Until then I hadn't told anyone what was going on. But as soon as the council man left I phoned some friends in Deal to tell them what had happened. They rallied, but what could they do? How could our new community be stopped from turning our new home into a living hell? Why couldn't they just leave our children alone? After all, the children never wandered on to anyone else's property and they never did anyone any harm. I talked and talked to all my old friends and decided that afternoon that we would have to leave, or I would leave the house in a wooden box.

Fred and I argued hammer and tongs. I told him we had to leave. I told him we would go to Wales, where we had always planned to move in the long run when the children were older. He was outraged. Why should we let 'them' bully us out of our new home? There had to be a solution and Fred decided that if we improved the house, made an extension for a dining-room so that we could use the existing one as a play-room, the children wouldn't have to play outdoors. At least it would solve one problem, although it would be expensive and was far from ideal. Whatever I wanted I could have had, within reason. He would have done anything to keep us all happy and to keep the family in that house. He insisted we should stick it out and show Margate that his family was made of sterner stuff than them.

But there was nothing Fred could have done to make that place bearable. Our lives continued to be made a misery, as a result of which I finally snapped. It's not often that I blow, but when I do, heaven help anyone in the area. The thing that always makes me more angry than anything else is when people have a go at my kids – I'm like a vixen, then. They can walk over me any time – if they dare – but not my kids. I can't even remember the incident which finally made me lose my rag, but Fred got the brunt of it, and I flung a cup at him. It missed but I told him that I was leaving and that if he felt so strongly about sticking it out, he could. By himself. All I could think was: sod the lot of them, Margate and Fred.

Days later – no, I didn't leave in the end – Fred and I made peace. He knew I was at breaking-point and so gave in. We got the address of an estate agent in Wales through *Dalton's Weekly*, only to discover that most of the houses were too expensive for us – until the details of one near Synod's Inn in Dyfed arrived. It had seven bedrooms, two bathrooms, a kitchen and a sitting-room and we could afford it, which meant that it had to be in terrible condition. But Fred, armed with a camera, went to see it the following day, stayed overnight in the van, and brought back the evidence. Just as I'd thought, it was in an appalling state. Mildew crept up the walls of all the downstairs rooms, rainwater trickled into the upstairs rooms through the leaking roof, and there was no hot water or heating unless you lit the Rayburn. Leaking windows and cracked drains let further dampness and stench into the house, and some of the walls weren't even plastered let alone wallpapered. I knew it would be quite a struggle, but I also knew that we all needed peace of mind or the family would fall apart. OK, so the roof was leaking; we'd use umbrellas until we could fix it. So there was mildew on the walls; well, we'd just scrape it off until the walls could be treated. We would manage.

We explained to the children that we were going to move again and those who could understand were very relieved. Finally Matthew, Ben and Eddie, who had been keeping a tight rein on their emotions, could tell us how unhappy they were and how much they hated Margate. Poor things – we knew how miserable they were, but they had been trying to spare us some pain by refusing to complain about their lot. They couldn't wait to leave, and they packed that day. God was with us. The house was sold on the day it went on the market. There were so many moments in those eight months when I'd lost faith in the love of God. I was sure he had deserted us but, looking back on it all, perhaps the episode was designed to remind us not to take things for granted.

The surge of relief was almost overwhelming. We were leaving a nightmare. I threw myself into travel arrangements, finding workmen and telling our friends about the move. They must come and visit us, they must not lose touch. Suddenly life seemed to have a future for us. The only thing which troubled me was the thought of leaving my daughter Lorraine and my two young grandchildren, Zoe and Jannine. Without hesitation Lorraine said she would give up her council flat to come with us. If necessary she would live in a caravan so that she could give us all the moral and practical help we needed. Once again we moved at the worst time of year – two weeks before Christmas – but I would have moved on Christmas Day itself rather than stay a day longer than we had to. Surely nothing would ever be as bad as that again.

At eight o'clock in the morning on 19 December, 1987 we loaded up the van with sandwiches of every description, bottles of pop, flasks of coffee, potties and nappies. We wrapped the children in overcoats, scarves and gloves, and drove away for ever. Fred was the only one of us who had been to Wales and here we were, about to make Wales our home. The van was alive with excitement.

The journey took seven and a half hours with only two stops, to give Fred a break and the children a chance to stretch their legs. Some of the children slept, others played with each other and all of them asked 'Are we there yet?' every twenty minutes or so. We sang songs, talked about our hopes for our new life, watched the countryside turn from the manicured Home Counties to the wild woods and hills of Wales. Finally the van took a sharp left down a small country lane and our eyes settled on our new home, Hafod-y-Bryn, which means 'barn on the hill'. It is a small farmhouse made of grey Welsh stone with a pebbledashed extension. To one side there is an old cow shed which we hoped to be able to turn into a playroom. But that was looking far into the future. Now we had to try to turn this ramshackle building into our home.

151

We were greeted by the woman from whom we had bought the house. It was three o'clock, we were stiff and tired, and she had not yet moved out. We went into the sitting-room, which was freezing and remained so despite the fire Fred lit because the previous owner's furniture was being ferried out through the sitting-room door into the garden. Matthew's face said it all. What have I let myself in for? Margate was bad enough, but this is terrible. At least Margate was warm. If he had had a home to go to in Kent I think he would have gone straight back there without unpacking – but there was no going back. But he never said a word, he just got down to unpacking the tea chests, which had arrived just ahead of us, and settling in the family. We had promised him that Wales would be better than Margate, but at that point I'm not sure he believed us.

We explored the house. Each room seemed colder than the last, broken pipes littered the rooms, the walls were waterlogged from broken loo pipes, none of the doors or windows fitted properly, woodworm and dry rot were rampant, but I felt at home, I felt happy: the house had a good spirit. By eight that evening, Fred had plugged in a small electric heater to lift the chill from one bedroom just enough to make it bearable for the night. Eddie, Ben, Lucy, Matthew, Simon and Fred slept there, while I slept in the sitting-room with Lorraine, Jannine, Zoe and Susan.

The following day we unpacked the essentials, put carpets down in the vain hope that they would make the house warmer, plugged electric heaters into every room, dug out changes of clothes for everyone and concocted strange meals in the microwave: bacon cooked in shifts, with cold baked beans because there was nothing to heat them on; we couldn't even find enough plates and knives and forks, so we had to take turns at the family trough! The Rayburn had an oven which could produce two kinds of food depending on its mood: raw or burnt. A few days after we had moved in it caught fire, with flames leaping around the kitchen of our new house. The children were bundled outside and the fire brigade called, lights flashing. We had made our mark on the local community. The firemen were kind souls who realized that the children had been badly scared. So when the fire was out they let Matthew and the rest of them play on the engine, turn on the siren and even help use one of the hoses, which gave them all great pleasure.

How different this community was from Margate. The day after we had arrived we found welcome cards pushed through the letter box. People called round to introduce themselves and offer help. But I think the most heart-warming thing to happen in the first week was arranged by our nearest neighbours, Lynne and Myra Davies, who own a farm and caravan site down the road. Two days before Christmas they invited us along to their caravan site community centre, where they had laid on a Christmas party complete with a Father Christmas for the children. Lynne and Myra told us they didn't want our children to miss out on Christmas just because we had moved. What a wonderful thing to do! What kind people! It is something we will never forget. It was the first kind gesture to us for nearly a year.

All our neighbours were the same. They left Christmas cards and holly on our doorstep. They invited us to tea. At last we had found a community of good, kind people who did not treat us like outcasts. We were three miles from the sea, and we were surrounded by magnificent countryside. I knew we were going to be very happy. I put back on the weight I had lost and Fred, well Fred just loves it. He started doing work he had never contemplated before: laying sewerage pipes and floorboards, and patching up the roof. Even now he is hard at work and there is still plenty to do, but that doesn't matter because we have come home.

Slowly, the children began to come out of their shells. Matthew loosened up and started to talk again and he and his brothers and sisters became a happy, united group once again. Even Susan stopped her occasional temper fits and learned to make a few more responses, like giving me or Fred a quick cuddle or leaning her head against my shoulder or even touching Matthew. It may not sound much but it's quite a step for her: physical contact is not easy for a child like Susan because she is autistic. No one seems to know much about autistic children and the experts give conflicting advice. But one thing I have noticed about all the autistic children I have come across is their inability to give or receive any physical contact. They live in a world of their own, you are not there for them. There are no real answers, so I just try to do what seems best for the individual.

Eddie has left school now and goes to a day centre for disabled people called Bronaeron, at Aberaeron, where he's involved in basket-weaving and rug-making. It may not be work to you or me but, as far as Eddie is concerned, it's work. He earns forty pence a day and it gives him a great feeling of achievement. The only time we are reminded of the Margate nightmare is when Simon, who will always be a confused child, shouts at the local farmer: 'Why are you so nasty to us? Why don't you love us?' The farmer, like all our neighbours, has been wonderfully kind to our family; at times, though, some echo of that miserable episode comes back to Simon, and for some reason he takes it out on the farmer.

Matthew, Ben, Simon and Susan go to Highmead, a lovely school seventeen miles away in a village called Llanybydder which takes in educationally subnormal

children as well as mentally and physically handicapped children. We decided to send Matthew there
because he is so far behind with his school work. It has
its own flock of sheep, tended by the children, and it is
set in twenty-eight acres of land. Right now they are
building an adventure play area in the shape of a ship,
an enterprising venture when you consider that all the
construction work is being done by children with
mental, physical or educational problems. Matthew
adores the school and he has already made lots of
friends. They have even been to a summer camp in
Morfa Nefyn in Gwynedd.

The move to Wales, on top of Matthew's new-found
confidence through surgery, has brought out a cheeky,
witty side. One day when life at Hafod-y-Bryn had
been more chaotic than usual he rolled his eyes in
mock horror, made for the door and shouted, 'Oh
God, it's a madhouse here – they'll have me like it if I
stay any longer.' And, when he helps the children
with the tea, he will say to Susan, whose coordination
is bad to say the least, 'Don't kill the sausage, cut it.'
Giggle, giggle. And when Lucy reaches to throw her
Ribena across the table he doesn't stop her but shouts,
'Timber – duck for the oncoming blackcurrant tree.' I
think his latest joke may end in tears: every time a
weight watchers' advertisement appears on the television he calls to Fred, whose waist measurements
don't bear thinking about, 'There's a great programme
on the telly, come and see,' and runs out of the room
before he can get a clip round the ear.

I cannot believe how well the children have taken to
their new life. Matthew and his brothers and sisters
speak a few words of Welsh, and the only episode to
have upset them so far is when a new-born lamb died
while Matthew was shepherd. There was nothing he
could have done, the lamb would have died whoever
had been there, but he took it very badly. Like all the

rest of the children he helps tend the garden where all the vegetables for their school meals are grown, but his favourite duty is still shepherding. Meanwhile his academic work is improving fast, and so with a bit of luck he will have caught up with his contemporaries in a year or so. Lucy goes off to Aberystwyth twenty-three miles away to a special school for young children, and they all arrive back at about four o'clock full of stories about their day. It's just like old times.

Matthew has had three more operations; Professor Jackson did two of them in England, at Springfield Medical Centre, Chelmsford, and the third back at the Mayo Clinic in the States. Slowly his ears are taking shape with skin from behind his groin. We are very proud of Matthew and so are all the people who have helped to raise money for him and who have come into contact with him. It is not the special surgery, or the fame, or the special attention Matthew has received over the years which makes him special to us. Matthew is a special person. Quietly and unobtrusively he helps us around the house and with the rest of the family. He doesn't have to, it's just a niche he has carved out for himself. He loves bathing little Lucy, although he has to strip down to his shorts to do it because she tends to fling cups of water at him! He will make high tea for the family with complete confidence and bustle off to the kitchen, without being asked, to make cups of coffee or tea for visitors. He loads up the dishwasher and helps me prepare meals. And he never makes a song and dance about helping, he just gets on with it. But over and above all the practical help he gives us, he has brought his own special spiritual qualities of kindness, love and fun to our family.

It would not have been surprising if all the media attention and the fund-raising activities had made him big-headed, but they haven't. He has an extraordinary inner peace which is clear to anyone who meets him in the flesh. But what strikes me above everything else is the way Matthew can bring out the best in those around him. Our love and pride in him grow every day and my only hope is that his real mum, whoever she is, has been following his progress and is as proud of him as we are.

All Futura Books are available at your bookshop or newsagent, or can be ordered from the following address:
Futura Books, Cash Sales Department,
P.O. Box 11, Falmouth, Cornwall TR10 9EN.

Please send cheque or postal order (no currency), and allow 60p for postage and packing for the first book plus 25p for the second book and 15p for each additional book ordered up to a maximum charge of £1.90 in U.K.

B.F.P.O. customers please allow 60p for the first book, 25p for the second book plus 15p per copy for the next 7 books, thereafter 9p per book

Overseas customers, including Eire, please allow £1.25 for postage and packing for the first book, 75p for the second book and 28p for each subsequent title ordered.